Breathe, Stretch, Write

LEARNING TO WRITE WITH EVERYTHING YOU'VE GOT

SHEREE FITCH

Pembroke Publishers Limited

Dedication

To the memory of friend Isabelle Scott, a soul who danced in the light and breathed and wrote with grace and joy. A teacher. A shepherd.

And to Lucinda LaRee: God-sister, yoga instructor, friend who taught me to breathe more deeply and brought Isabelle to our writing group.

© **2011 Pembroke Publishers**
538 Hood Road
Markham, Ontario, Canada L3R 3K9
www.pembrokepublishers.com

Distributed in the U.S. by Stenhouse Publishers
480 Congress Street
Portland, ME 04101
www.stenhouse.com

We acknowledge the financial support of the Government of Canada through the Book Publishing Industry Development Program (BPIDP) for our publishing activities.

We acknowledge the assistance of the Government of Ontario through the Ontario Media Development Corporation's Ontario Book Initiative.

Library and Archives Canada Cataloguing in Publication

Fitch, Sheree
    Breathe, stretch, write : learning to write with everything you've
got / Sheree Fitch.

Includes index.
ISBN 978-1-55138-256-2

1. Creative writing (Elementary education). 2. Creative ability in children.
3. Breathing exercises. 4. Stretching exercises. 5. Hatha yoga. I. Title.

LB1576.F58 2010   372.62'3   C2010-903827-4

Editor: Kat Mototsune
Illustrations: Harry Black
Cover Design: John Zehethofer
Typesetting: Jay Tee Graphics Ltd.

Printed and bound in Canada
9 8 7 6 5 4 3 2 1

FSC
www.fsc.org

MIX
Paper from
responsible sources
FSC® C004071

Contents

Preface: Warming Up

Breathe, Stretch, Write is a book of exercises for teachers who want to explore and embrace a whole-being approach in the teaching of creative writing in their classrooms. Breathing exercises. Stretching exercises. Writing exercises. Why this combination?

Once upon a time, there was a little girl who had a teacher who encouraged her students to write. This was somewhat amazing because, at the time, creative writing was not common practice in classrooms. That little girl discovered writing was magical and challenging and joyful. That teacher used everything she had to generate excitement for her students by creating a safe and stimulating learning environment. I was that girl. I grew up to be a writing maniac. A published author. A rhymester. A lifelong learner.

My inspirational teacher's name was Bea Goodwin. How could I make that up? Be Good and Win. In Be-Good-and-Win's Grade 2 class, we did daily calisthenics, isometrics. Some of you might remember those exercise words, or maybe you just remember the teachers who had you stand, push back your chairs, wiggle and stretch. We sang songs like "If You're Happy and You Know It (Clap Your Hands)." Belting out tunes was good breath work. We took what we might call "brain breaks": lights were turned off, heads placed down on desks. We listened to the radio! Mrs. Goodwin read aloud to us. I suspect her teaching was just the common sense classroom survival tactics of a Grade 2 teacher, not a learning strategy or anything mandated in the curriculum or by outcomes. Be-Good-and-Win's philosophy was simple—each student was special; we all possessed gifts she would nurture in ways she could. And healthy bodies = healthy minds.

A few years ago I was asked to be on a policy panel that was studying the effects of media on childhood obesity. I was alarmed and shocked at the increases in childhood diabetes and childhood obesity presented in that study. Around the same time, I was doing readings in schools in the US where gyms had been turned into cafeterias and recess was a thing of the past. No recess! I couldn't believe it. How does cutting gym period help children stay healthy? I found that this was happening in some schools in Canada as well. What a disconnect! How do we expect children to learn when energy is low, bodies are dragging, and minds are numbed?

I knew how essential exercise and physical activity was in my own life as a writer. I understood my creative energy depended upon my mental *and* physical well-being, and I was already using movement and basic yoga in the writing classes I offered. So I started studying and integrating more of the physical into my teaching. The idea to put some of this exploration in book form happened because teachers and students urged me to share some of what I've learned using a body-centred approach.

Happily, as this book goes to press, things look more hopeful. A child's right to play, health issues, children's fitness and the link to learning are making the news. That is a good thing for all of us.

So, to begin at the beginning.

There is really nothing new under the sun. This is a book of common sense. In one way, this book is about retrieving the forgotten givens, basics like this: your brain needs oxygen and exercise to work well and grow strong, and authentic writing is rooted in the body.

Mrs. Goodwin knew what she was doing when she said, "Stand on your tip toes and reach for the sky." Or when she turned off the lights and had us rest our heads for a few minutes of silence. Mrs. Goodwin was my *permissionary*; i.e., someone who gives you permission to dream your wildest dream, follow your heart, use your head, and share whatever gifts you've got. For me that meant becoming a writer and teacher.

My hope is that this book offers an approach and becomes a tool that allows busy teachers to be permissionaries to their students. I hope that the ideas offered here revitalize and inspire and keep opening up the channels of creativity so that learning to write is exciting and fresh. If it helps teachers be permissionaries to themselves in the development of their own writing through their Breathe/Stretch/Write practice, even better. Arguably, the best teachers of writing are teachers who write and keep stretching themselves. Teachers who model themselves as writers and as people who are ever learning are perhaps the biggest inspiration of all.

Here I can only echo the words of Brenda Ueland: "Everyone is talented, is original and has something important to say." I have seen proof of this in all corners of the world, in people of all ages and stages of literacy. Writing is only one way of saying, of telling our stories. Let it be a way students can find faith in their own voices and faith in themselves.

So… begin with each breath, work through the body, and feel how "the ground is found." Write without fear and discover how writing that reveals authentic voice and vision can come forth!

> *Physical fitness is not only one of the most important keys to a healthy body, it is the basis of dynamic and creative intellectual activity.*
> —John Fitzgerald Kennedy

Introduction: Moving Up to Writing

What is this—writing as an extreme sport?

No, not exactly—but, yes. *Breathe, Stretch, Write* is a book of ideas and inspiration, a resource book for teachers of writing and anyone who wants to deepen and explore their own writing practice by integrating breath, body movement, and fun in their creative-writing journey. Still, you don't have to be an Olympic athlete, nor will you be asked to stand on your head—unless you want to—and there is no Sanskrit requirement. This is not a how-to-do-yoga book, even though it provides some basic yoga postures as inspiration and as points of departure.

This book is an invitation to approach the creative-writing process intentionally through the body, a whole-being approach to inspire the inner writer in every one of us. Writing is a process of discovery and, by bringing our whole being to the work, we can make writing a safe, exciting, joyfully challenging experience for even the most reluctant writer. This book is based on personal, experiential truths:

- Working with breath and body grounds and focuses the mind.
- Writing is a physical exercise as well as a mentally challenging and intellectually demanding activity.

Maybe writing is metaphysical, but physical? Isn't that a *stretch*? Not if you think about the physicality of writing for a moment. Whether you are using a pen and paper or a computer, you are sitting still, holding your neck and head a certain way, using your arm, hand, wrist, fingers.

I asked Elie Cossa (a veteran fitness instructor and personal trainer at City Fitness in Washington, DC) to explain to me what happens in my body when I write. Here's what she wrote back to me:

> The muscles used would differ a bit depending on the position when writing or typing. I am going to describe it as if someone is at a desk doing so, but will do some parenthetical notes on someone lying back with a notebook or something like that. I am going to write from the core of the body moving down the arm, for the sake of organization.
>
> 1. Longhand
>
> As one would be leaning forward slightly with arms resting on a table, there is use of abdominal and back stabilization muscles. The erector

This book happened because of teachers and writers who urged me to share some of what I've learned as a writer using a body-centred approach. Many of the exercises are ones I've offered in professional development workshops and W.I.S.E. Words writing courses over the past 20 years.

spinae, trapezius, latissimus dorsi, and rhomboids would support the back of the body. The transverse abdominus, rectus abdominus, and internal/external obliques would support the front of the torso. Though the shoulders and arms should fall relatively relaxed as the arms rest on the desk, the serratus anterior and pectoral muscles will engage slightly, particularly as the person begins to write, to assist in applying pressure.

(If one were seated holding a notebook, there would be more pulling from the supporting arm and most likely a slight lean to one side. The posture support muscles would be pulled on the one side and smushed on the other, causing a variation in use. The arm holding the notebook would use the biceps and gripping muscles in the hand. One would also use the muscles in the neck a lot more in a seated or lying position, so the levator scapulae and trapezius would kick in more.)

The rotator cuff helps to move or rotate the arm from the shoulder joint. The anterior deltoids, pectorals, posterior deltoids, biceps, and triceps help slide the arm forward and backward. In most situations the rotation and sliding happen simultaneously as the hand moves up and down the paper. (If seated or lying, one would do the same movement, but from the hand holding the notebook instead of the one doing the writing.)

The pronation muscles of the forearm—the ones that turn the palm inward—are the pronator quadratus and pronator teres muscles. The brachioradialis is a helper to get the arm into a pronated position too.

The same muscles mentioned for grip strength would hold the writing implement, but finger bending is primarily the flexor digitorum superficialis and flexor digitorum profundus. Flexion of the wrist, bending the wrist toward the palm, occurs using the flexor carpi radialis, flexor carpi ulnaris, and palmaris longus. Extension of the wrist in the opposite direction uses the extensor carpi radialis longus, extensor carpi radialis brevis, and extensor carpi ulnaris.

2. Typing

The same posture muscles, of course, would apply. People tend to use the neck and shoulders a little more at the computer because of the height of the desk and the keyboard and mouse position. The head position also differs because the person is looking up or ahead as opposed to down; again, more neck and shoulder use.

The only differences when it comes to the arms are the following:

- More pronation at the forearms because the hands turn all the way over to type
- Less range of motion regarding flexion and extension of the wrists, as the hands tend to stay in a more fixed position. But, because there is downward pressure as you type, you are still using those muscles and tension in the top of the wrists as the muscles help support and hold, but in a more isometric way instead of in a moving way.
- More use of the flexion of the fingers, again because you need a different kind of strength and dexterity to push the keys down
- The only use of the gripping muscles would be when using the mouse.

Whew! No wonder those of us who write for long stretches complain of back aches, and shoulder, wrist, and neck problems! So, if writing does make all these very physical demands on the body—not just the mind—what if we worked *with* our body in the actual writing process? Look at it another way. Picture your thoughts in your head and your feelings in your heart meeting at the shoulder and having a conversation: what do you think? what do you feel? what shall we write about? Once the decision is made, imagine the idea traveling down the arm, out of the hand and pen onto the paper. A long journey. Sometimes for one word! Literally, an out-of-body experience.

Think what we are requiring of our bodies every time we sit down to write, every time we rewrite. Like any extreme sport, writing is not for the faint of heart or weak in body. Why not keep fit for the voyage? Why not Breathe, Stretch, *and* Write?

A few years ago, the physicality of writing was brought home to me in an unusual way. I had been working really hard on a manuscript and not working nearly as hard as I usually did at the gym. I started suffering extreme pain and cramping in my feet and toes. I went to the doctor, who questioned me on my shoes and sneakers and such. "Same as always," I said. Still the pain and cramping persisted. I wondered if some sort of arthritic condition was beginning. One morning as I was sitting at my desk, focusing on writing a very intense scene, my husband walked in the room and said, "Look how you're sitting!" Then he pointed downward. I was barefoot with my legs wrapped around my chair, which was bad enough—but worse, I had my big toe and the one next to it in a death grip around the leg of that chair. "That's it!" my husband said. "That's why your feet hurt after a day of writing."

If anyone had ever told me I could get toe and foot injuries from writing, I would never have believed them! So now, I wear my sneakers when I write. *If You Could Wear My Sneakers*, you'd know that writer's cramps are real.

Breathe, Stretch, Write for All

Breathing with intention increases blood flow, improves circulation, and sends oxygen to the brain. When breathing, we revitalize our energy and wake up our nervous systems. When we engage our bodies in intentional stretching, we dwell in our bodies and free our minds. We create space—not only in our diaphragms and chests, but in our busy minds. Refreshed, bodies humming with new energy after breathing and stretching, we can begin or return to the page.

Establishing the habit of writing, of writing freely and frequently, of viewing oneself as a writer, leads to confidence and joy in writing. Over time, this yields positive results in longer pieces, in pieces intended for others and/or evaluated in assignments or examinations. The integration of breathing, moving or stretching, and writing cultivates mindfulness, clarity, focus, and self-awareness.

The prompts and exercises in this book are designed to spark the writer within. The writing generated may or may not be revised to become finished pieces. This is writing as an exciting, fun exploration, using the breath and body so authentic voices and visions of each writer will emerge.

This is all fine and good, my writer- and creative-self says, but my teacher-self says, "Yes, but we still need goals." The goal is to inspire, guide, coach, coax, relax, and release authentic voices and visions onto the page. The voice and vision of each writer is as individual as a fingerprint. Loud, quiet, messy, juicy, passionate, sober, playful, earnest—real writing emerges when the environment is safe. Breath unites the body and mind. Writing through the body yields amazing results in writing. Fun is a goal! And the physical and mental health benefits are just as important as the skill of learning to write effectively.

As a writing teacher for almost 20 years, I've heard people say, "But I can't write," or "I hate writing," or "I am afraid." Or, the one that made me saddest, "I don't have any imagination." *Where along the way did those people begin to feel this way about themselves?* I wonder. My first challenge in any class always seems to be addressing and conquering that fear and insecurity in participants and showing them that, yes indeed, they do have imagination. I see those same people write heart-stopping lines after some guidance.

In writing classes, I approach the writing process simply: by working and playing with the four elements I call my W.I.S.E. Words workshop. It is mainly the *S* in the W.I.S.E.—i.e., *Senses* seeing, hearing, touching, tasting, smelling—that leads people to find their authentic and original voices. Working with the senses is mentally writing through body. For example, which *feels* colder, snow or snow down the back? Connecting with the sense of touch makes a reader almost feel that snow. Any time a sensory detail is used, a reader is placed that much more fully in a scene or captivated that much more intensely by an image. I've seen even the most reticent writer liberated by understanding through their bodies and senses. The body often knows in ways our minds cannot grasp.

What is W.I.S.E.? All the writing exercises I've used in workshops over the years are organized around the four major elements of writing or the W.I.S.E. Words workshop approach. W.I.S.E. is an acronym to remember the four major tools in any writer's toolbox:

Words
Imagination
Senses
Experience

Precluding those with disabilities, we all have our five senses; we all have imagination, words, and experience. We are all wise. Learning to listen deeply, to trust one's inner wisdom, is part of the journey of writing. Learning to listen to one's body is also a matter of intention and practice.

W.I.S.E. Words and Breathe, Stretch, Write are not formulas, but a being-in-the-moment approach that facilitates one kind of writing experience. Students gain confidence in themselves as writers and produce unique, fresh pieces when writing is done in the spirit of exploration, instead of just for an assignment or grade. This approach is also a gentle way to stress

- use of concrete and specific language over general
- that showing and telling are both important
- how metaphors are both powerful and individual
- that we are all original
- that we have tools, strategies, boundaries
- that keeping the pen moving will lead you somewhere
- that play does not mean "silly"
- that we are writers when we write

An experience in Canada's North inspired me to take the writing-through-the-body idea a step further. I was teaching in the Arctic in an innovative land-based literacy program called Somebody's Daughter. By day the participants were sewing to reclaim the traditions of their elders. At night we gathered in the tent, and it was my job to midwife their stories, both oral and written. By the second day, we were all complaining of sore muscles and backs. We started stretching. When we did a version of the pose that in yoga is called Warrior One, we called it the Inukshuk. When we leaned over, we called the pose the Leaning Inukshuk. There was a lot of laughter. That was the night we really started opening up to each other. From that point, the writing was more honest, more imaginative, and more sensory.

When I returned Washington, DC, I enrolled in a core-strength training program and yoga-teacher training course, so the next year I'd have more to offer when we stretched and wrote. I never intended to become a certified personal trainer or teacher of yoga, but I wanted to learn as much as I could and see how it might all connect. I certainly wanted to learn more before integrating my ideas fully in writing workshops. I experimented over the following few years in every writing class I gave.

The results were exciting. Breathing, Stretching, and then Writing seemed to free the most inhibited writer. Writing can be exciting and fun—and, yes, anyone can do it.

How to Use This Book

In one sense, you can consider each page of this book a ready-made workshop. You can use one or any number of exercises to offer in a once-a-week workshop; you can use the whole book as a guide for creative writing clubs and to create homework assignments; or you can simply flip this book open to any page and find an exercise to spark a five- to ten-minute activity in class. Ideally, this kind of spontaneous invitation to move and write can become a welcome break between other activities.

The idea is for writing to flow without worry of right or wrong, without fear of punctuation, spelling, or getting it right. This is writing for the self. If the writer wants to share orally, even better; if an idea is generated for future revision, terrific. Doing the same exercise will yield different results every time.

The Breathe/Stretch/Write format is simple:

- Breathe: In this book, every exercise begins with breathing.
- Stretch: Then a move or Stretch, a body-connected exercise, is given.
- Write: After each Stretch, one or more Writes, or writing exercises, appears.

Also sprinkled through the book are personal moments I have had in working and playing in my world of words; discoveries or reflections I think worth sharing; writing samples; inspirational quotes; and Fitchness Tips for writing.

From Reading to Writing

Read, read, read! This is the first piece of advice most writers give to those who want to write, or to write more effectively. We learn to write by writing—and by reading.

I suggest teachers or workshop leaders plan to introduce a piece of writing before beginning each of the Breathe, Stretch, Write exercises in this book. A poem, a quote, a chapter, a paragraph, part of a story or a piece of an essay—give students words you like, words that touch, inspire, or give an example of excellence in writing. It can be something funny; perhaps something provocative. A file folder overflowing with random pieces of inspired and inspirational writing can be an inspiration for all the writing in a class.

Guess what—writing is never perfect in the first burst. That's what revisions are for!

Creating the Creative Space

We are energetic beings. Creating uses energy. Taking care of and being mindful of my body, paying attention to my breathing and bringing this to my writing, has yielded fresh discoveries and changed my writing. I started being able to find the focus, clarity, and concentration to consider tackling different genres. I wrote my first novel, *The Gravesavers*. I took more risks. I grew more confident. Writing really demands a kind of confidence that most of us do not come to easily. The more I set my intention and integrate body work and breath in my own writing practice, the more I realize that they are essential to my overall well-being. This nurtures and benefits my creative life, sharpens my powers of observation, opens up blocked pathways, and improves my reasoning skills. Bodywork and breath work feed my brain. All of this encourages pathways to release energy!

Emotional Space

Sure, the world out there is tough and competitive, but the seeds of creativity are tender and sensitive, and need to be watered and nurtured if they are to sprout and bloom forth. Not everything everyone writes is going to be "good" according to some objective standard of excellence. But if we are to encourage the storyteller and writer within everyone, and honor authentic voice and vision, we first need to create a safe space. Like doctors, teachers are asked to do no harm. How fragile is the poet in everyone. Go gentle into that good write!

I have long been aware of the importance of creating an emotional space to write. Before I went off to university to study children's literature at the graduate level, a well-intended friend—in a very friendly manner—challenged my decision to study children's literature. "Why study children's books when you could study great literature?" he asked. To me, children's literature was the most important literature. After all, wasn't that where children developed their love of books? So I got a tad upset. Actually, I started ranting about my belief that children's literature was worthy of scholarly study, even though at the time it was still called "kiddie litter" in some academic circles. When my pal saw how upset I was, he backed down a little. I had to take more than a few deep breaths.

"Okay," he said. "I get your point, and maybe after you've studied children's literature at the Masters level you can come back and answer a question I've had for a long time."

"What's the question?" I asked.

"Well first I have to tell you a story," he said. (See, everyone is a storyteller!)

"I'm all ears," I said. We sat at my kitchen table and this is the story he told.

Several years ago I was returning home from doing research in Ireland. Halfway over the Atlantic the plane started experiencing engine difficulty. Now, it's a funny thing when people are in a time of crisis. You start to see how different everybody is. Some people began to pray. Some people began to cry. Some people wanted a drink. Others wanted information. And some people like me got very, very quiet and still. Unfortunately, the woman sitting next to me decided to use me as a pinching pillow. She kept kneading the flesh of my arm between her fingers until my skin turned white, and whimpered every time we hit a bump. I tried to remain calm, even though I realized my research was in my briefcase under the seat and all my efforts in my wee quest for truth might possibly end up in the Atlantic Ocean. Obviously we finally made it all the way to Newfoundland.

And when they got us to the airport they herded us into the bar. I pulled up a seat and ordered a whisky. Unfortunately, the arm grabber pulled up the seat next to mine. "I just want to thank you," she said, "for being so nice to me. I know I really lost it there for a while." At these words of praise I puffed myself up and said to her, "Well, yes, I never knew I could remain calm in such a time of crisis." At this, the arm grabber threw back her head and laughed. Laughed hysterically. For a second, I thought she might be in a state of shock, and then she said to me, "Don't you know what you were doing?" And I said, "Yes, I was reading my magazine." In between fits of laughter she told me, "First of all, that magazine you were reading was upside down. And this is what you were doing. You were rocking back and forth a little like this." She showed me. "And all the while, you were saying 'hey diddle diddle, the cat and the fiddle, the cow jumped over the moon' and 'James James Morrison Morrison Weatherby George Dupree'. The whole time," she said, "You were reciting poems and Mother Goose."

My friend looked at me that day and asked me with great seriousness, "So what I need to know, when you're all done studying children's literature and have your Masters degree, is why, when I was closer to death than I've ever been in my entire life, I started to recite Mother Goose and A.A. Milne.

I was smiling by this time. "I don't need my degree to answer that question. You went back to the poetry of your childhood because it took you to a safe place." In the moment of the telling of the story or the poem there is the creation of a safe place.

Above all else, the ideal creative space is a safe place. This means creating conditions for a writing workshop experience or environment that builds self-worth and confidence, increases the joy in working and playing with words, improves literacy and fluency skills, and integrates body and movement with fitness awareness. This can be done in a way that eliminates comparison with others' work, fear of failure, and the sense of rightness and wrongness.

One of the most effective ways to do this is for the guide or teacher to participate as a member of the class/workshop, **to do the exercises and model oneself as a writer ever learning**. Sharing the work is never forced on anyone, but is part of the fun—listeners are encouraged to say what they like or what surprises them most about a piece that is read. Comparing texts using "like and different" not "better and best" help create a non-competitive atmosphere: use comments like, "It sounds to me *like* William Blake's poem 'Tyger'" or "How is this character *different* from the prince in the Paper Bag Princess?"

> **Like *and* different *are quickening words, brooding and hatching,* better *and* best *are egg sucking words, they leave only the shell*.**
> —Ursula LeGuin

Physical Space

Ideally, there is a separate space in your elementary classroom where you can move away from the desks. Writing can be done on the lap—not on laptops. Working outdoors is a nice change, even if you return to the classroom to write. However, creating this separate space might not be possible: therefore, many of the stretches and activities can be done beside chairs and desks, and no special

Needless to say, but too important not to say: We need to keep reminding ourselves and others that the words we choose, when we give feedback to work shared orally and in group, are crucial. A respectful room of listeners honors the writer. This also helps each writer develop an editorial eye and establish standards of excellence in written work.

Fitchness Tip

• This space is yours to create. Think of space as spaciousness. Consider how to efficiently store yoga mats, blankets, pillows; a place for journals, pencils, pens, pencil crayons, extra paper, etc.

rearrangement of the room is necessary in most cases. In terms of time, a good parameter for the stretching component would be from three to ten minutes.

For older grades, these workshops might be best done in the gym, in a music room, or at home. That way, work can be done on yoga mats, with notebooks close by.

Breathe

Smile, breathe and go slowly.
—Thich Nhat Hanh

Even though no one can live very long without breathing, I didn't learn how to breathe properly until I was in my forties. If there is one thing I hope to teach my grandchildren it is this: Understanding how to use your breath is one of the best tools you have to help you cope with life's unpredictability. Your breath is one of your best friends. Inhale. Meet your breath friend! Exhale. So long! Inhale. Hello, again!

Breath is the link between body and mind. It is brain food.

Breathing lessons can get overly complicated; there are different kinds of breathing—calming, energizing, brain breathing—and fancy names for breathing. For the purpose of this book, when the instruction *Breathe* is given, it means this:

1. Always breathe in and out through your nose.
2. Place your hand close to, but not on, your belly near your navel. Inhale. As you do, gently push your belly toward your hand.
3. Exhale. Pull your belly in. Imagine your navel touching your spine.
4. Do this three times.
5. Return to normal breathing.

So, in the beginning is the breath— *not* the word. If we remember the words *respiration* and *inspiration* come from the same Latin root word, the connection between breath and mind is obvious. Traditionally breath was considered the carrier of prana; i.e., life force or spirit. We find energy and inspiration in the intentional, mindful use of the breath.

In this book, all the writing exercises begin with a cleansing breath. Then, by coordinating breath as the poses are executed, we open up even more physically and emotionally, and experience increased or heightened awareness back in and through the body. Think of this loop: breathe, move, breathe, open, breathe, relax, breathe, write, breathe, release. When we write from this body place, we are already deeper in ourselves and closer to authentic voice and vision. I love this quote from Nicephorus the Solitary, an ancient mystic:

You know that our breathing is the inhaling and exhaling of air. The organ that serves for this is the lungs that lie round the heart, so that the air passing through them thereby envelops the heart. Thus breathing is a natural way to the heart. And so, having collected your mind within you, lead it into the channel of breathing through which air reaches the heart and, together with this inhaled air, force your mind to descend into the heart and to remain there.

What if we really do open our hearts by breathing deeply? According to yoga master Eric Shiffman, intentional breathing also increases our sensitivity. In *Yoga, the Spirit and Practice of Moving into Stillness* he writes:

> You'll notice how holding your breath dulls your feeling-sensitivity, and how letting the breath flow freely and deeply increases it. You'll notice how your breathing actually fans the feeling, increasing and clarifying it, heightening your ability to sense yourself. Learning to feel and feel deeply is one of the most important learnings in yoga. Proper breathing will directly enhance your feeling sensitivity.

I would add that feeling deeply is one the most important learnings in writing and in life. We need empathy to write fully believable characters, to articulate our deepest truths, and to live in community with others—to seek to understand them even if our differences are great.

Even the most confident of us could benefit from breathing lessons. Who doesn't want to feel calm and a sense of inner peace? It takes work! Walk, dance, laugh, drink, and be merry—but breathe! What a useful thing to remind and share with each other.

I was giving a speech in front of large crowd and I had all my notes on index cards. I wore my good-luck scarf and had rehearsed in my head, but knew I would be nervous. When I am nervous, I talk even faster, which is scary because even at normal speed people call me Lightning Lips. So, because I wanted to remind myself to slow down, on the back of each index card I wrote *Breathe* in big letters. Early on in my speech, I flipped an index card and read it out loud. "Breathe!" I shouted out to the whole room. Oops! "That was a reminder to me, not an instruction to you!" I explained. We laughed. And laughter forced me to breathe. It worked! I slowed down…until the next page.

Stretch

In this book, *Stretch* means move, means pose, means body activity.

The instructions for each stretch are simplified for our purposes. They could be very detailed and taken slowly if we were in a body movement or yoga class; however, the aim here is to move through the breath and through the body and the senses to get to the writing. The focus is still more on the writing than on the body and the movement. It is not a gym class, so each of the stretches should take only three to ten minutes before you move into the writing exercise.

Having said that, it is still important to realize that we bring the mind and set intention to execute the pose, to dwell deeply in the moment in the body. This is preparation for and part of the writing process, the part of the writing process we concentrate on to help us discover, uncover, and release the stories and images hidden inside.

Concentrating on the movement, and not just "performing" the move, will ground the writer and create space for fresh creative energy to flow.

Here is where we get doing, not thinking. Just as the Breathe cleanses and renews and warms us up in spirit, the Stretches ground us in the body and are the warm up for the writing. Very often the name of the pose itself will suggest images, and the visualization process begins, consciously or unconsciously. Kneeling and making our hands move like waves over sand, do we see ourselves at ocean's edge? Inhabiting and being attentive in our bodies, using our breath as

Fitchness Tips
- Beware—you might find yourself clearer than ever, yet at the same time less understood by others who cannot see that breathing deeply is a path worth choosing.
- The real trick is how to learn to use the breath in such a way that it dissipates anger, anxiety, and other difficult emotions in the moment.
- Relax. You know yourself. For some, it is no big deal. For others, an effort.

Remember: the breath links body with intention.

Fitchness Tips
- All of these movements and body exercises are adapted from somewhere else—and are just suggestions.
- Be creative and use your own body-centric approach to inspire a creative writing exercise.
- Build up a repertoire of moves.
- Take turns having students initiate and model the Stretches, even inventing names for them, and write from there.

we execute the pose, we enter the imaginative and creative zone—a dream space, a kind of waking trance.

I have offered these exercises to people aged eight to 88. For students in younger grades, the play aspect of movement is stressed, while with older grades the philosophy and connections to well-being—mental and physical health and fitness—can be stressed. Many of the exercises can be given as home assignments or to individuals.

This book is written with the awareness that a range of physical abilities and challenges are present in every teaching situation. It is up to the teacher's discretion to work with sensitivity—introducing, adjusting, modifying the exercises in *Breathe, Stretch, Write* so that using this book is a positive experience for all.

Sally Smith (founder of the Lab School) always said, in terms of teaching kids with learning disabilities (and I think all children) that you start with what you the child knows and has experienced. The body is the beginning.
—Amy Young

Fitchness Tip

• To be open to the energy in the room, to allow yourself to be led by intuition, is a leap worth taking. Still, teach with intention. Know the pose.

The link between the Stretch and the writing exercise might be a stretch (pun intended) and not always obvious, so feel free to adjust, change, or modify to suit your needs. In workshops, I teach by getting inspired in the moment by what has just been shared orally. There are sometimes obvious spinoffs. If you see each suggested activity as a blueprint, not a carved-in-stone step-by-step strategy, you can be more deeply in the moment as a teacher. And you can have more fun, as you loosen up. Yes, you can be literal—have a cat stretch lead to writing a cat piece—but in my experience a nuanced approach is far more interesting.

Write

A long time ago I wrote with abandon—the sheer joy of letting the words flow loosely from my pen. Then I got published and found myself paralyzed! I'm not exactly sure why, but for a while I thought everything I wrote had to flow from my pen perfectly, even though I knew writing *was* rewriting and revision. I knew I had to learn to kill my inner critic in order to get anything down. So I began to play. I wrote again as if no one was watching or would ever see it. I gave myself time limits and did a lot of these exercises myself, and still do (sometimes mid-book if I am stuck). Tongue twisters are good for this.

I began to notice in workshops with students that the same inner critics and demons of doubt were present in nearly everyone. The expectation that we somehow have to get it right the first time around seems to be in everyone—along with the fear of not being as good as others. Try as I might to encourage everyone to see how the rawness of our first drafts contain seeds of greatness and authentic voice, it still makes people vulnerable to write—and even more so to share—even if we know a piece needs further work. Finished writing requires rewriting and only a few writers I've met revise word-by-word as they go along. Most writers get it out, then go back to refine. So the fear of our writing not being good enough as it comes out needs to be conquered. Get it out! Get it down! Working with fun and ease, knowing we have another chance at greatness and perfection, releases energy. And indeed great things do come.

> *There is no question that a nourished, exercised body makes using the mind for creative thinking easier.*
> — Jill Badonsky, M. Ed.

Sometimes, from my first-burst writings, ideas for characters or plays or books develop.

So, let go of desired results and be fully engaged in the process! When we loosen up in our bodies, there is liberation. This can lead to risk-taking on the page. Timed exercises create a sense of urgency, a flurry of energy. In my classes I call the results "first burst" writing.

Remember to stress:

- There is no right or wrong!
- More on the page is not the goal.
- It is not a competition
- Everyone knows they will be interrupted before they are "finished."
- Everyone has the right to pass and share when comfortable.
- This writing is something to look at, reflect on, and maybe go back to at some later point to revise and complete.
- The workshop leader or teacher should do the exercise as well and be willing to share from time to time.

Fitchness Tip
- Never throw anything away, especially those lines you love best. If you believe in what you've written, it could just well be you are waiting to write the story they belong to. Recycling is a good thing! There are many kinds of letting go!

The creative prompts offered here are intended to inspire a flow. It is writing generated for the sake of writing, but it can always be integrated into other lessons already planned. For example, a science lesson on worms could lead to crawling on the floor and being a worm, and then writing in first-person from the perspective of a worm as it tells us all we need to know about wormness. Similarly, sitting with eyes closed and imagining a hurricane or other current event could lead to powerful writing for older students. Simply breathing, shrugging, and releasing before any writing, even an exam, can help with focus, memory, and clarity. At the same time, the Write exercises are prompts into the work the student chooses to write—in other words, a way to uncover the stories that might be buried deep inside and are just waiting to get out.

The exercises are clustered around standing, seated, reclining, moving, and group poses—but often the division is just that. Find the moves and poses your classes love the best and switch up the exercises to suit the subject. For example, Butterfly (page 58) can be a playful or solemn image—the classroom situation that steers the Write often sets the tone of the piece created.

The prompts will suggest fiction, poetry, verse, plays, songs, but also some creative nonfiction, personal anecdotes, and persuasive writing—as many kinds of writing as you can dream of. Because the emphasis is on first-burst writing or what might be called "pieces" of writing, at this stage the emphasis is on focus and process, not form and results.

Invitation to Inspiration
Take a deep breath
IN
Come IN!
Now Breathe Out
Begin! LET THE WORD RUMPUS BEGIN!

What would you tell Sheree about how moving and stretching affects your writing?

- If you have distracting thoughts in your mind, some poses help erase all those thoughts and let you get new ones.
- You can write down the feelings you get, like, if the pose was relaxing or painful, you write down those emotions.
- It helps you think free.
- It helps us focus on writing. It might be painful, relaxing, or it might help you concentrate… mostly painful!
- Stretches can help us be relaxed. You can feel the words coming down into your hand.

— *From Kristen Moore: Grade 4 Teacher, Bloomfield Elementary*

Before you start working with your students, let's give the process a try:

1. Open your writing journal to a fresh page. Have pen and paper ready and close by.
2. Stand up.
3. **Breathe:** inhale, exhale three times. (See breathing instructions on page 16).
4. **Stretch:** Raise your arms. Clasp your hands. Turn your hands so your palms face the ceiling. Keep your shoulders away from your earlobes by drawing your shoulder blades down your back.
5. **Breathe:** inhale, exhale three times.
6. Release your arms. Dangle them by your sides. Wiggle your fingers.
7. **Write:** Everybody's body has a story. Sit down and write for ten minutes a piece entitled "A Short History of Me and My Writing Buddy Body."
8. Stop. Read. Reflect. Star the lines or a turn of phrase that surprises you most. Save.

The Standing Exercises

We stand in line at the grocery store and the bank. Some people stand in food lines and unemployment lines. We stand first thing when we get out of bed, and are happy to flop down at night. We stand back from things, stand up for things. We take a stand. We under-stand. Standing is an outstanding accomplishment.

All of the following poses begin with the idea that standing, taking our stand in the world, is not easy or mindless: it can be one of the most challenging things to do. Think about Bob Marley's "Stand up for your Rights." Listen to "Stand by Me."

Begin an unrhymed poem called "I Understand" and fill in the blanks. What do you stand for? Can you find a funny twist on standing up for things? *Stand up for lemons! They're always in a squeeze.*

Seriously, when we stand in these stretches, we stand with intention. We are trying to keep head up, neck straight, spine straight, shoulders away from the earlobes and pulled down the back, shoulder blades separated, and other limbs relaxed—including your chin and jaw!

We are trying to find our ground, hold ourselves steady. Anchor. Root. Maintain an erect posture, not a lazy slump forward. Think upwards, onwards. Walk with a book balanced on your head!

Lots going on! Can you relax with all this standing at attention?!

1. Stand on Your Own Two Feet

In yoga this is Mountain pose or basic standing pose. While resting in Mountain pose, imagine you are strong like a mountain. Imagine you have the vision of someone who is looking down from the mountaintop. Finding your balance is a lifetime high-wire journey.

Breathe

1. Always breathe in and out through your nose.
2. Place your hand close to, but not on, your belly near your navel. Inhale. As you do, gently push your belly toward your hand.
3. Exhale. Pull your belly in. Imagine your navel touching your spine.
4. Do this three times.
5. Return to normal breathing.

Stretch

1. Stand with feet hip-width apart, toes lined up.
2. Feel your feet firmly planted in the ground.
3. Balance your head on the vertical centre line of your body.
4. Drop chin forward slightly.
5. Arms are by your sides with elbows slightly bent, hands soft and slightly cupped.
6. Roll shoulders back and away from earlobes.
7. Keep your gaze soft and slightly forward.
8. Relax.

1. LIST
   - Make a list of the five most important things in your life.
   - Pretend you are five years old. Make a list of five most important things.
   - Pretend you are 88. List five most important things.
   - Pretend you are a dog. List five most important things.
   - Look at the lists. Are there things in common? Discuss.
   - Pick one thing from any list. For five minutes, write about that one thing.
   - Stop. Ask if anyone would like to read what you have written. If not, move on to the next exercise.

2. FIND YOUR MOUNTAIN
   - In your mind, picture a place. Find your mountain. Rest there a bit.
   - Write about someplace you'd like to visit and why.

Fitchness Tip
- This is a good grounding exercise. Why would we get excited writing about something if it was not important to us? If we do not care about it, why would a reader?
- This is a good exercise to use if stuck in a story. Identify the five most important things in a character's life or in the plot at this moment. It's amazing how this helps dissolve writer's blocks.

In 1998, I was invited to the country of Bhutan, a country nestled in the Himalayas, to do some teaching and readings. We travelled from one end of the country to the other. At times it really did feel like we were in heaven because we were driving through clouds. The serpentine roads were narrow and there were no guard rails. It was a long way down—a very long way. I often got out and walked because the car was creeping along and I felt more at ease with my own feet on the ground. One day we ended up at place where we got out and my husband pointed to a sign. I read: *You are at the highest point.* We took a picture. It was one the highest points of my life. A dream came true—I was in the Himalayas. This is often my image when I am in Mountain pose. Other times it is the hill behind my house where we tobogganed when I was a kid. It was a mountain to me.

2. The Frame

Socrates said the unexamined life is not worth living. To write is to observe, to examine. Part of what we need to do is stop and look—to freeze-frame an image in our minds or register an emotional connection in our body. So we begin with looking at ourselves. And out from ourselves.

Breathe

1. Always breathe in and out through your nose.
2. Place your hand close to, but not on, your belly near your navel. Inhale. As you do, gently push your belly toward your hand.
3. Exhale. Pull your belly in. Imagine your navel touching your spine.
4. Do this three times.
5. Return to normal breathing.

Stretch

Fitchness Tip
• Find a poem you like. Frame it!

1. Stand heels together, toes touching, hands at your sides.
2. As you inhale, raise your hands over your head.
3. Bring your hands down so you cup your ears with your hands, elbows out to the sides.
4. Frame your face with your hands.
5. Move your hands to the top of your head. Interlace your fingers
6. Exhale and lower your arms back to your sides.
7. Breathe three times.

Write

OUT OF THE FRAME

• Everyone gets a painting or picture to look at. Study it, pass it around.
• Write for five minutes.
• These prompts might be useful: What is the story you found in photo or painting? Can it be dramatized? Can you add dialogue to the scene by imagining conversation of the people (if any) in the piece?

3. Gathering Flowers

Moving your legs to a wide stance shifts energy and circulates breath in different ways. Take a few minutes just to feel the difference in this pose from Standing on Your Own Two Feet (page 22). There is a sense of expanding outward. Writers try to expand our imaginations, expand beyond the limits of our own selves and perceptions, and see beyond our world. Take time to focus on this feeling of expansion. After this expansion, swooping to the ground is restful. The real joy is folding into the image in this pose. From firm stance, to expansion, to the swoop, you visualize gathering up in your arms as many flowers as—and whatever kinds of flowers—you can. That is what we want to do with first burst writing, to gather up words we can arrange the way we want and when we are ready, to offer them, give them to someone to read. A word bouquet!

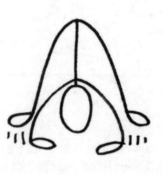 

Breathe

1. Always breathe in and out through your nose.
2. Place your hand close to, but not on, your belly near your navel. Inhale. As you do, gently push your belly toward your hand.
3. Exhale. Pull your belly in. Imagine your navel touching your spine.
4. Do this three times.
5. Return to normal breathing.

Stretch

1. Stand in Standing on Your Own Two Feet (page 22).
2. Step wide, with your legs as wide apart as possible.
3. Bend at the waist and dangle your head.
4. Pretend to gather bundles of flowers, sweeping your arms side to side.
6. Straighten up.
7. Release, throwing flowers into the air.

Write

1. IN MY GARDEN
   - Write for five minutes on the title "In My Garden."
   - Variation: Write about planting and growing things you'd never expect to find in a garden.

2. UNRHYMED GIFT
   Write a piece called "This Poem Is for You." Start with these lines:

   I'm putting things you love
   Inside this poem…

4. Starfish Hands

You can do this pose standing or sitting. We use our hands for writing. The words travel through our arms and out from our hands, whether we are typing or writing. This is a hands-on handout! Handy exercise to remember when you have cramped hands. Just rubbing hands together generates heat. Bringing awareness to the hands like this, we know we are working with energy.

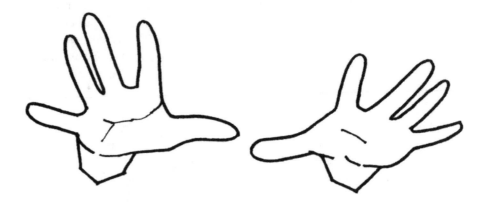

Breathe

1. Always breathe in and out through your nose.
2. Place your hand close to, but not on, your belly near your navel. Inhale. As you do, gently push your belly toward your hand.
3. Exhale. Pull your belly in. Imagine your navel touching your spine.
4. Do this three times.
5. Return to normal breathing.

Stretch

1. Bring your awareness to your hands.
2. Clench fists.
3. Unclench fists.
4. Make starfish shapes with your hands.
5. Relax hands.
6. Make loose fists.
7. Shake your hands loose.

Write

1. WORD HANDS
   - Trace your hand on paper.
   - Outside of the hand shape, write words that have to do with hands (clapping, touching, tapping, sewing etc.) When you are done you have a hand made out of words.
   - Write a hand poem on the inside of the hand.

2. STARFISH

Write for five minutes about a starfish; your writing can be rhymed or unrhymed.

Starfish

Starfish why?
Oh, do tell me why

Do you have five arms?
That's three more than I.

But the question it begs is
Are two of them legses?
—*Cameron Lamond*

Cameron Lamond is a correctional officer, a father of twins, and a poet.

All parts of the body which have a function if used in moderation and exercised in labors in which each is accustomed, become thereby healthy, well developed and age more slowly, but if unused they become liable to disease, defective in growth and age quickly.

—Hippocrates

5. Try Angles

This classic pose symbolizes—and takes—strength. But it is also about feeling balanced and then changing the balance by changing the orientation of the body. Often when we write we have sense of what we are doing, and then inspiration comes and we are thrown off balance, off our original course. It is much easier to go with the flow of the unexpected idea or inspiration if we know that underneath we have ground from which to explore. Go ahead. Tip over. Then give some tips of your own on what works for you when you write.

Breathe

1. Always breathe in and out through your nose.
2. Place your hand close to, but not on, your belly near your navel. Inhale. As you do, gently push your belly toward your hand.
3. Exhale. Pull your belly in. Imagine your navel touching your spine.
4. Do this three times.
5. Return to normal breathing.

Stretch

1. Stand with feet wide apart.
2. Bring arms out straight to the sides, parallel to the floor.
3. Point your right foot to the side at a 90° angle; point your left foot slightly to the right.
4. Shift hips very slightly and, following through the arm first, bend your body to the right, bringing your right hand as close as possible to the outside of the right foot.
5. Bring your left arm up so that it is in a straight line with the right arm.
6. Look up at your left hand.
7. Hold as long as it's comfortable.
8. Come up slowly.
9. Repeat on the other side.

Write

Use this exercise as a warm-up.

- Hold up a pen; ask what it is. It's a pen, right?
- Hold it sideways and pretend to brush your teeth with it. Now what is it? Toothbrush.
- Pretend you're sewing with the pen. Now what is it?
- Pass it around the circle: everyone has to use the pen as something else. Everyone can guess.
- Don't worry if everyone can't come up with an idea; just pass on the pen, and if a person thinks of one it can come back.
- Go once around the circle and maybe more, as long as folks have ideas or until you are ready to move on.

Writing is not only seeing something as it is but seeing what it can become. Your body as a triangle. A tree branch as a witch's claw-like hand scratching the sky. Writing is the act of transformation.

2. TRIALOGUE

For five minutes, work on a dialogue piece between three people entitled "The Triangle."

Decide on your tone ahead of time: funny, intense, antagonistic, relaxed. Consider these questions:

- Who are your characters? Name them, give them ages and occupations.
- Where does the trialogue take place?

Fitchness Tip

- Pass the pen is an old drama game. We use our imaginations: a pen is not a toothbrush, but you guessed it because you imagined and have experienced what it is—you know what brushing teeth looks like because you've done it .

6. Rag Doll

Writing often means seeing things from as many angles as possible. When you bend forward from the waist, release everything you can, breathing into the forward ragdoll-limp feeling. Sense your body going from straight and tight to curved and loose. This is reversing the stand position while we stand, and it shakes things up (like the triangle pose on page 28). It helps us let go in writing process. Relax and release. Write without thinking, without overthinking. Go ahead. Loosen up. The worst thing that can happen is bad hair when you straighten back up!

Breathe

1. Always breathe in and out through your nose.
2. Place your hand close to, but not on, your belly near your navel. Inhale. As you do, gently push your belly toward your hand.
3. Exhale. Pull your belly in. Imagine your navel touching your spine.
4. Do this three times.
5. Return to normal breathing.

Stretch

1. Stand with feet slightly apart.
2. Raise hands slowly above your head.
3. Bend forward slowly from the waist in a curling motion, dropping your head first.
4. Unfurl each vertebrae until you can go no further.
5. Keeping your arms beside your ears, let your body hang forward by its own weight for a few seconds.
6. Grasp your ankles—or whatever you can comfortably reach—and dig your chin into your neck.
7. Exhale as you slowly uncurl and come up.

Write

UPSIDE DOWN

Using all five senses, write for five minutes beginning with "I woke up in the middle of the night, and everything seemed upside down…"

Here is a poem about upside-downness.

Chinese Jack-o'-Lantern Plant
Your pumpkin-orange blooms
decorate my autumn walk;
those puffed and papery lights
glow on lampposts of green stalk.
But I think it's funny
that your bright and sunny tops
blossom in the shape of
upside-down tear drops.
—*Carol-Ann Hoyte*

Carol-Ann Hoyte is a Montreal children's poet whose work has appeared in Canadian, American, British, and Australian children's magazines.

Loosen up! Sometimes I play a game of spoonerism in schools. A spoonerism is when the beginning sounds of words get switched. It is named after a Reverend Spooner, who often mixed up his words like that. I call it Lipslippery Language. "Mood gorning, goys and birls," is an example of a spoonerism. Eggs and bacon becomes "beggs and acon." "Cowl of bereal" is a bowl of cereal (not cold beer!). Usually, I give examples by playing with the names of the students: Trevor Smith becomes Srevor Tith, Gillian Hobbs becomes Hillian Gobbs. Once, when I was doing this (with around two hundred Grade 4 students), one boy raised his hand and asked me what my name would be in the Lipslippery Language. "No one ever asked me that before," I said, "and I never even tried. Me, I would be Feree Shits." It took ten minutes for the whole auditorium to stop laughing. How I remember those long minutes, red-faced at the front of the room, embarrassed but laughing despite myself. The teachers laughed so hard I thought they'd fall off their chairs. Mistakes happen. Can we laugh at ourselves when they do?

7. Just Bee

Write and read aloud. Why? To hear the word music. The voicebox is a tool for the writer. This exercise helps work out the vocal chords. But write and say it out loud! Learn to love the sound of your own voice. Writing is about finding your voice or the many voices within.

Breathe

1. Always breathe in and out through your nose.
2. Place your hand close to, but not on, your belly near your navel. Inhale. As you do, gently push your belly toward your hand.
3. Exhale. Pull your belly in. Imagine your navel touching your spine.
4. Do this three times.
5. Return to normal breathing.

Stretch

1. Stand in Stand on Your Own Two Feet pose (page 22).
2. Begin to make a buzzing sound. Let sound come through your teeth.
3. Fly! Feel the buzz in your whole being.
4. Relax.

Write

1. BUZZ

Invent a word starting with *B* or a *Z*. Write for five minutes using the word.

2. RHYME TIME

Write a poem with your invented word as the title.

> **Zorp**
> I never ever saw a zorp.
> I think the zzorp's extinct.
> I think the zzzorp's a zorpish sort.
> Now tell me what you think!

8. The Painter

Words are the colors a writer paints with. Sometimes we see the scenes before we write them. Creating scenes can be like rolling a movie in your head. This exercise is meant to bring out the inner artist in everyone. Try to go from the pose to writing without thinking too much. Turn the imaginary paintbrush into a pen. Go ahead make a colorful splash—a mess on the page. (Try this with colored chalk or markers.)

Breathe
1. Always breathe in and out through your nose.
2. Place your hand close to, but not on, your belly near your navel. Inhale. As you do, gently push your belly toward your hand.
3. Exhale. Pull your belly in. Imagine your navel touching your spine.
4. Do this three times.
5. Return to normal breathing.

Stretch
1. Hold one arm as if holding a palette.
2. Using the other hand, pretend to dip a paintbrush in the paint on the palette.
3. Swirl your painting arm in circles as if painting on large canvas.
4. Make smaller circles as if adding minute detail.
5. Repeat on the opposite side.

Write

1. COLOR YOUR WORLD
Decorate or describe a room for five minutes. Your room can be however you want it to be: messy or organized; ugly or beautiful.

2. YOU ARE THE ARTIST
Draw/doodle a cartoon and caption that you think makes commentary on something current in the news.

9. Walking

Like the simple act of standing, walking becomes mindless; it is an almost involuntary activity. But when we become mindful and aware of what we are doing when we walk, what happens? Walking is actually the way we move from one place to another. Walking is a small miracle. Step by step we get somewhere. So it is in writing, word by word we get somewhere. We make a sentence. A sentence becomes a line in a poem or a paragraph in a story. Step by step we are getting somewhere—to the story we want to tell, the poem we want to create.

Breathe

1. Always breathe in and out through your nose.
2. Place your hand close to, but not on, your belly near your navel. Inhale. As you do, gently push your belly toward your hand.
3. Exhale. Pull your belly in. Imagine your navel touching your spine.
4. Do this three times.
5. Return to normal breathing.

Stretch

1. Begin standing in Stand on Your Own Two Feet pose (see page 22), with hands loosely at your sides.
2. Step forward. Feel the ball of the foot as you take each step. Take ten paces.
3. Return to the beginning position and Stand on Your Own Two Feet.

Write

1. COUNTRY WALK
   - Imagine you are walking in the country. Walk on sensory alert.
   - Write for five minutes, recording the sounds, colors, sights, smells you can imagine. Try a landscape portrait. Remember to include tiny details.

2. A SOUVENIR OF YOUR WALK
   - Go for a walk and pick something up.
   - Return to your place, and place it in front of you.
   - Let it talk and write for five minutes.

3. JUST WALK
- Run or march on the spot.
- Sit down and write.

While I was walking today on my country road (with a stick my husband made for me), a fox jumped out of the ditch, crossed the road, looked at me and sat down. I said, "Fox, I'm not turning back today. You and me share these roads, okay? I'm coming through." I banged my stick. He gave me a rather bored look and slowly disappeared into the bushes. I walked on, kind of nervous, but passed the spot where he had vanished. Then I thought how my imagination is like that fox sometimes—full of surprise. Sometimes I'd like to turn back because it seems hard or scary, but if I walk toward it slowly, with intention, it ends up being okay—and even kind of amazing. "I share the road with my friend the fox…" strikes me as the first line of something.

10. Tree in the Wind

Writing is showing and telling; it is a balance between the two. Writing is imagining and re-collecting, a digging down and a reaching outward. This pose allows us to find balance, root ourselves, and expand. Embody a tree. What if you were a tree? *What if…*—two of most powerful words a writer has to begin creating a world, or a person has for finding hope and opening up to possibility.

Breathe

1. Always breathe in and out through your nose.
2. Place your hand close to, but not on, your belly near your navel. Inhale. As you do, gently push your belly toward your hand.
3. Exhale. Pull your belly in. Imagine your navel touching your spine.
4. Do this three times.
5. Return to normal breathing.

Stretch

1. Stand with feet hip-width apart.
2. Raise your right knee.
3. Place the sole of your right foot on the inside of your left thigh, keeping your right knee extending to the side.
4. Maintain balance.
5. Bring your hands, palms together, centred in front of your chest. This is called "heart centre."
6. Extend your hands above your head.
7. When you're ready, open the arms to create a V shape.
8. Stand for three seconds.
9. Slowly lower your hands back to heart centre.
10. Slowly lower your right foot to the floor.
11. Repeat on the left side.

Write

1. WHAT IF...
   - Write ten *what if...* questions. For example: What if I were a tree? What if I lived in a cloud? What if it never snowed?
   - If you want to share, read your ten sentences aloud. You could even call this a poem of sorts.
   - Take one of the *what if...* questions. Try to answer it. Write for five minutes. See what happens.
   - Variation: Write a character sketch of someone in your family tree.

2. LOCALI-TREES
   - Research the trees that grow where you live.
   - Write a poem, including as many species names as possible.

Storm Surge
Beech, birch, ash, cedar
Fir, maple, oak
I'm glad I'm not
A tree today.
That's no joke.

---

11. Look Out, Here I Am!

This is called Warrior pose in yoga, but I like this name better. It reflects the release of essence and energy for purposes of writing. There is a kind of fierceness and courage needed to confront the empty page. And certainly we, as people, are not all happy-happy nice-nice all the time. We are a swirl of emotions and feelings and thoughts. This is a stance that says, "Ready or not, here I am. All of me." Imagine the pen at the end of your arm in this pose. Think of the pen as a sword—and even mightier than the sword. You are the one in control. (Do not be afraid of getting ink on your hands!) This is a great pose for feeling strong and in control.

Breathe

1. Always breathe in and out through your nose.
2. Place your hand close to, but not on, your belly near your navel. Inhale. As you do, gently push your belly toward your hand.
3. Exhale. Pull your belly in. Imagine your navel touching your spine.
4. Do this three times.
5. Return to normal breathing.

Stretch

1. Stand in Stand on Your Own Two Feet pose (see page 22).
2. Step with your right leg forward. Bend that knee.
3. Turn left foot slightly out.
4. Inhale, raising arms overhead or straight out to your sides. Keep your ears away from your shoulders.
5. Feel your feet on the ground and hold firm. Breathe in and out.
6. Repeat on the other side.

Write

1. TANTRUM POEM
Rage on the page. Write about what angers you! But use your words and senses carefully.

2. BLURB BACK
Write a blurb for the back cover of a book you will write someday.

3. BAD GUY
Write about your favorite bad guy (or girl) in stories you have read.

4. GOOD GUY
Research and write about someone who fought for a good cause and won.

When I was writing the Gravesavers, my character Minn is pretty angry about a situation in her family. Part of the way she copes with her rage is to run. When she is really mad she "cusses' in a geographical way. "Tatamagouche!" "Nipisiquit!" A few times she uses plant names in Latin. It's easy to love characters who are loveable, but it's more interesting to create characters who, like ourselves, don't always act and behave perfectly. Everyone knows how hot and uncomfortable anger feels. How we learn to handle that emotion is what matters. Minn learns a little about that—so does the character Jake in my senior teen novel *Pluto's Ghost*. I'm still learning.

> *Most people never run far enough on their first wind to find out they've got a second. Give your dreams all you've got and you'll be amazed at the energy that comes out of you.*
> —William James

12. Runner's Start

There is something about an empty page that can make me feel like I'm at the beginning of a race—or a marathon. But I don't always know where I am going or where the finish line is. This pose can convey the energy, excitement, and terror of facing the blank page.

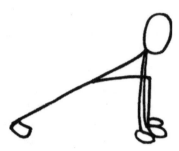

Breathe

1. Always breathe in and out through your nose.
2. Place your hand close to, but not on, your belly near your navel. Inhale. As you do, gently push your belly toward your hand.
3. Exhale. Pull your belly in. Imagine your navel touching your spine.
4. Do this three times.
5. Return to normal breathing.

Stretch

1. Stand.
2. *On Your Mark*: Squat.
3. Kneel on one knee.
4. Place hands shoulder-width apart on floor or ground ahead of you.
5. Keeping one knee on the floor, bring the other knee to your chest and place that foot on the floor.
6. *Get Set*: Raise the other knee, lifting your buttocks. Keep your eyes ahead.
7. Hold *Get Set* for several seconds. Breathe.
8. *Go*: Shout "Go!" and explode from *Get Set* position as if ready to race.
9. There's been a false start. Begin again.

VARIATIONS
- Instead of step 8. Go, relax and release.
- If you are outside, sprint a little way.

Write

1. STORYTELLING
- Find objects. Put them in the centre of the group.
- Have students who want take a turn pick up an object and start to tell fantastical story about it. "Once upon a time". . . can be the beginning.
- The object gets passed on and next person continues story.

2. RUNNING
Write about a character who is in a hurry to get somewhere. What are the obstacles in his character's way?

13. The Fencer

Words, words, words. Finding the exact right word is challenging. Back and forth, back and forth, shuffling up and down and sideways, until…there—aha!—that's the word. Pinned it down. Ah! Satisfaction. You know you have it when you feel that "got it!" feeling in your belly.

Breathe

1. Always breathe in and out through your nose.
2. Place your hand close to, but not on, your belly near your navel. Inhale. As you do, gently push your belly toward your hand.
3. Exhale. Pull your belly in. Imagine your navel touching your spine.
4. Do this three times.
5. Return to normal breathing.

Stretch

1. Start in Mountain pose.
2. Exhale into Rag Doll bend (see page 30).
3. Bend your knees. On inhale, step left foot back.
4. Bend your right knee to form a right angle.
5. Lean your torso on your right thigh.
6. Come up with your arms pointing up alongside your ears. Keep your torso lifted.
7. Extend your right arm straight out and face in that direction.
8. Hold and release.

VARIATION

- When in the pose, pretend you are in a sword fight—shuffle back and forth.

Write

1. TALK SHOW

You are Oprah. Or Ellen! Who's on your show today? Why? Write an introduction for your guest.

2. OUR GUEST TODAY

You are being interviewed. Why? What have you done? Pretend you are explaining to a studio audience what makes you famous; e.g., how you survived in the wilderness, how you invented something, etc.

14. Downward Dog

Writing is digging deep. Digging in. Digging things up. Downward Dog is a basic yoga position that some find restful and others challenging. It is a good all-over body stretch. It demands a grounding, a letting go, learning to breathe in inverted position, a sense of your inner thighs, and moving your shoulder blades down your back. Think of becoming a human upside-down V. Work on this until it becomes a restful pose for you—effortless.

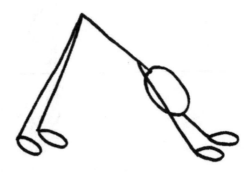

Breathe

1. Always breathe in and out through your nose.
2. Place your hand close to, but not on, your belly near your navel. Inhale. As you do, gently push your belly toward your hand.
3. Exhale. Pull your belly in. Imagine your navel touching your spine.
4. Do this three times.
5. Return to normal breathing.

Stretch

1. Stand with your feet flat on the ground.
2. Slowly bend forward at the waist and bring your hands to the ground.
3. Lean your hips back and buttocks up until you are in an upside-down V shape.
4. Try to keep your feet flat on the ground, but bend slightly in the knees if it gets uncomfortable.
5. Breathe into the posture.
6. Release and come up to standing.

VARIATION
- Bark!

Write

1. DIG DEEP
If you had only one story to tell, what would it be? Who would it be for?

2. THE CASE OF THE DIGGING NEIGHBOR
Write in the voice of someone who sees a neighbor dig and bury something in his or her backyard. Solve the mystery.

15. Half Moon

This is a challenging pose and it takes a lot of practice—just like a finished a piece of writing takes more than one draft. Try to have fun with the pose safely. I think these guided writing exercises shine a light on ideas and imaginations, and the moon has long been associated with imagination and a truth different from that seen under the full light of the sun. When you go on to rewrites and revision, you move more into your head and away from your body, with its sensory impressions and felt emotional connections. These first sensory impressions hold a truth unique to each writer.

Breathe

1. Always breathe in and out through your nose.
2. Place your hand close to, but not on, your belly near your navel. Inhale. As you do, gently push your belly toward your hand.
3. Exhale. Pull your belly in. Imagine your navel touching your spine.
4. Do this three times.
5. Return to normal breathing.

Stretch

1. Begin in Stand on Your Own Two Feet pose (see page 22).
2. Move into Try Angles pose (see page 28) on your right side, with your left hand on your left hip.
3. Inhale as you bend your right knee.
4. Slide your left foot forward.
5. Reach your right hand forward just above the little toe of your right foot.
6. Press your right hand and right heel into floor as you straighten your right leg.
7. Lift your left leg parallel to floor.
8. Rotate your torso to the left.
9. If you feel comfortable, raise your left arm above your head.
10. Hold as long as it is comfortable. Breathe. Release.

Write

WHO ARE YOU?

- Write a personal metaphor for you at this moment. For example: *I am a salmon swimming upstream. I am a limp piece of celery.*
- Try three and end with this one: *I am a writer!*

The Sitting Exercises

Someone once said that writing happens when you apply the seat of the pants to the seat of the chair. In other words, you can dream all you want, but the only way to write is to do it. Unless you've got a laptop rigged to a treadmill (I know some writers who do!), chances are, you will be sitting in a seat on your seat to write.

Just as we stand unaware of what we are doing with our bodies, we usually just sit without thinking. Seated poses done with intention make us aware of the alignment of the spine, head, and neck, while engaging the lower body and working in new ways with breath and the diaphragm.

Taking our seat means grounding ourselves into the floor (or earth) in a position of readiness, partial repose, and receptivity. It is a good place from which to start to dream. And then—yes—to do.

The mind's first step to self-awareness must be through the body.
—Alexander von Humboldt

16. Sit Down and Shush

This classic pose is great for relaxation. It is amazing how a small act of adjusting your sitting bones on the floor or slightly opening your mouth and feeling your tongue on the roof of your mouth can relax your whole jaw. The *shush* sound is good to experiment with—make softer and harsher shushing sounds. Do this about three times as a group and then wait in silence. Even animals respond to the *shhh* sound and, for humans who are always chattering in our minds, it can help still the babble or at least slow it down. Let breathing become relaxed and easy. Gently rest the eyeballs by lowering the eyes and letting the eyelids almost close or close. I like imagining a rope tied to the tip of my head and, when I start to slouch, I see myself being gently tugged a little straighter. It helps me not round my shoulders. Relax but don't get body lazy! I confess, I have fallen asleep sitting up while trying to meditate.

Breathe

1. Always breathe in and out through your nose.
2. Place your hand close to, but not on, your belly near your navel. Inhale. As you do, gently push your belly toward your hand.
3. Exhale. Pull your belly in. Imagine your navel touching your spine.
4. Do this three times.
5. Return to normal breathing.

Stretch

1. Sit down on your behind. Wiggle yourself comfortable.
2. Cross your feet at the ankles.
3. Cup your hands on your knees.
4. Breathe. Keep your neck straight.
5. Lower your gaze three feet in front of you and continue to be mindful of breath.

Write

1. RHYMING NAMES

Play with names around a circle: e.g., Margaret Wargaret; Sheree Berry; Jess Guess etc.

This is a simple wordplay game but it is important. The naming of things is the claiming of things.

2. NAME GAME
- After playing with names for a few minutes, open journals and invent a name, first and last. Here are some sample names to get you started: Mr. Grumble, Fiona Fairweather.
- For five minutes write, creating that character.
- As always, when you are done, whoever wants to share can share.

3. EXPLAIN A NAME
- Write for five minutes beginning with these lines:

> The door opened. In walked Rad Leblanc.
> "Hey, Rad, how ya doing?"
> Radish Leblanc sighed, sat down, and said, " It's been quite a day."

- As you write think of the traits someone called Radish might have.

I take as much care naming my characters as I would a baby. I find names in name books, telephone directories, and the credits after a movie. I usually look up the origin and meaning of a name. If I'm going to be with a character for a long time, I want to like their name, and it has to be appropriate for the character. The name game is not just a game. It is about the right words and the sounds they make. The first poem I ever wrote was in Grade 2 when Mrs. Goodwin said we could write a poem about our names. She put my "Itchy Fitch" poem in the school fair. Watching the reaction of people that day, their body language—they smiled after reading—I realized words had power to connect and reach and touch another. I was hooked.

4. ACT A POEM
- Find and share a copy of a poem you love.
- Act out the poem with your body.

> *I took a great workshop at the Kennedy Center a couple of weeks ago called Poetry off the Page in which we were taught a poem through using our bodies to act out one motion per line, without ever seeing the poem in print. The poem became a part of our bodies and from there we were asked to write our own poems using some prompts. Having used our bodies, it was much easier to come up with metaphors from the physical world to represent our ideas.*
> —Amy Young, teacher at the Lab School, Washington DC

17. Cleansing Breath

This is a way to increase awareness of breath in the sitting position. Breathing while sitting is a different sensation from breathing when standing. You have to work a little harder because, when you are sitting, you diaphragm is squeezed—think of it as being like a kinked-up hose. Experiment with seeing the energy and breath in your mind as color. Inhale blue and exhale grey. See what happens. Imagine a shape to the breath. What shape do you see? Round and light? Solid and dark? Is it hard to imagine? Breathe and release!

Breathe

1. Always breathe in and out through your nose.
2. Place your hand close to, but not on, your belly near your navel. Inhale. As you do, gently push your belly toward your hand.
3. Exhale. Pull your belly in. Imagine your navel touching your spine.
4. Do this three times.
5. Return to normal breathing.

Stretch

1. Sit in comfortable cross-legged position (see page 46).
2. Inhale deeply, pushing the abdomen out.
3. Exhale, bringing the navel in towards the spine.
4. On the next inhalation, breathe through the mouth.
5. On the next exhalation, say, "Ah" three times.

Write

1. SONG WRITERS, ALL!

Pretend you can win a million dollars by coming up with song lyrics. Play! Sing!

2. LOCKED IN!

Imagine being shut in a room or trapped underwater. Try to create panic on the page.

3. FRESH AIR

- Research and write about air pollution.
- Write a piece about fresh air.

18. Opening a Window

Sometimes we get stuck—in life or on the page. We write ourselves into boxes or corners, or simply stop ourselves from seeing beyond the immediate word or sentence or dilemma we are facing. I love this pose for reminding myself that sometimes you just need to get up, open up the window of your mind, and look out. Get ready to bring in some fresh air. Amazing how the brain is invigorated and new possibilities appear.

Breathe

1. Always breathe in and out through your nose.
2. Place your hand close to, but not on, your belly near your navel. Inhale. As you do, gently push your belly toward your hand.
3. Exhale. Pull your belly in. Imagine your navel touching your spine.
4. Do this three times.
5. Return to normal breathing.

Stretch

1. Sit in relaxed cross-legged position (see page 46).
2. Bring your hands up to your shoulders, palms up, fingers pointing out, and elbows to the sides; your arms form a straight line with your chest.
3. Slowly raise your hands, resisting the motion all the way up.
4. Stretch your arms straight and then lower just as slowly, resisting on the way down. Breathe normally.
5. Repeat a few times.

Write

OUT THE WINDOW
- Begin writing a piece of entitled "Out This Window" or "From This Room."
- Then play with different windows and rooms: the window in a police car, the window of a train; a room in an old-age home; etc.

19. Snuffy Stuff

The sense of smell is one of the most powerful senses we have for triggering memory and emotion. Have fun with this. Focus on the facial muscles it takes to scrunch and unscrunch the nose and feel the jaw. Laugh! It's all in the name of breathing.

Breathe

1. Always breathe in and out through your nose.
2. Place your hand close to, but not on, your belly near your navel. Inhale. As you do, gently push your belly toward your hand.
3. Exhale. Pull your belly in. Imagine your navel touching your spine.
4. Do this three times.
5. Return to normal breathing.

Stretch

1. Wrinkle your nose as if sniffing, perhaps smelling something kind of bad.
2. The bad smell hits you. Wrinkle your nose harder.
3. Say, "Eeeuw!"
4. Repeat.
5. Breathe normally.

Write

1. MEMORABLE SMELLS
   - Write for five minutes about your favorite smell and what memory it brings to mind.
   - Write for five minutes about an unpleasant smell.

2. SMELLING ALL DAY
   - Spend the day paying attention to smells.
   - Write five minutes about one smell and what was going on when you smelled that smell.

3. THE SMELLY DAY
- Spend the day paying attention to smells.
- Write a piece called "The Smelly Day."

"I need more stinky in line three," said the voice on the other end of the line. That was my editor. We were on a deadline. So much pressure. We worked for an hour to come up with something stinky for that poem. Finally we settled on the line *there's skunk breath on the breeze*. It worked. But I couldn't help saying to the editor that day how lucky we were to have the work we did. Some people have important life-or-death decisions to make every day. My work as a storyteller is not earth-shattering and no one's life depends upon it—except maybe mine. I take my work seriously, but I love what I do and know really, when it comes down to it, I am lucky—privileged—to have such a stinky problem.

There are no days in life so memorable as those which vibrated to some stroke of the imagination
—Ralph Waldo Emerson

20. The Blade

Sharpen our pencils and minds, and sharpen the image on the page. Think of slicing through all the cluttered stuff to get to what you want to say simply, clearly, concisely.

Breathe

1. Always breathe in and out through your nose.
2. Place your hand close to, but not on, your belly near your navel. Inhale. As you do, gently push your belly toward your hand.
3. Exhale. Pull your belly in. Imagine your navel touching your spine.
4. Do this three times.
5. Return to normal breathing.

Stretch

1. Sit in a relaxed cross-legged position
2. Bend your elbows and bring them up to the side, fingertips touching in front of your chest.
3. Draw your shoulder blades together as if you're holding a pencil between them. (You might want to try this with a partner!)
4. Hold the pose for 10 seconds.
5. Release the pose slowly. Shrug your shoulders a few times.
6. Repeat a few times.

Write

1. ME IN ONE WORD
Think about and write one word to describe yourself.

2. A STORY IN FIVE LINES
Write a five-line story. Make sure everything you want to happen is there.

3. PORTRAIT OF A PERSON
- Pick someone you love.
- Describe them using your senses, telling something specific this person did or does that makes that person unique—the concrete details that are the most telling about who that person is. Remember the clothes the person wears, the food the person eats, physical traits the person has.
- It works well if you address the person as *you*: e.g., "Grandmother, your hands are bent with arthritis now and you find it difficult to sew" or "Son, you are a wiggly worm, a bouncing monkey."
- Add a last line—"And you love me."—to make it a gift for that person.

21. Reach for the Sole

Writing takes us places we do not expect, and often asks us to stretch beyond our comfort level and take risks. Some people think writing connects us with something we might call "soul"—this exercise connects us to sole! We can understand the process as reaching out slowly, as slowly as this pose. Respect our bodies, listen to ourselves.

Breathe

1. Always breathe in and out through your nose.
2. Place your hand close to, but not on, your belly near your navel. Inhale. As you do, gently push your belly toward your hand.
3. Exhale. Pull your belly in. Imagine your navel touching your spine.
4. Do this three times.
5. Return to normal breathing.

Stretch

1. Sit with your legs extended out front.
2. Bring your arms straight out to the sides and up over your head.
3. Inhale and draw the spine up long.
4. As you exhale, begin to come forward, making your body hinge at the hips.
5. On each inhale, extend the spine, and on each exhale, come a bit farther into the forward bend. Keep the neck as a natural extension of the spine. Try not to round the back.
6. Take hold of your ankles or shins, whichever you can reach. If possible, grasp the sole of your foot.
7. Breathe. Release.
8. Repeat with the other leg.

Write

1. APPRECIATE MY FEET

Keep examining your feet. Where have they taken you or where have you traveled? Write for five minutes.

2. GETTING AROUND

Write about someone who cannot walk. Why can't this person walk? How does this person get around? What does he or she feel about that?

3. FOUND ON THE GROUND

Go outside and walk, looking only at the ground. Come in and write a piece called "Found on the Ground."

22. Chopsticks

Let your fingers do the talking. Assume your seat but bring attention to the hands. Maybe review Starfish Hands (page 26). Focus on the fingers, the base, the knuckle, the fingertips. Writing requires fine motor activity. This is harder for some of us than others, and it can interfere with the writing process. I'm left-handed so I've had to learn to make friends with my hands in a lot of ways. I still prefer longhand writing. Think about what your fingers do for you every day. Play the old game Rock Paper Scissors. Then write on that paper.

Breathe

1. Always breathe in and out through your nose.
2. Place your hand close to, but not on, your belly near your navel. Inhale. As you do, gently push your belly toward your hand.
3. Exhale. Pull your belly in. Imagine your navel touching your spine.
4. Do this three times.
5. Return to normal breathing.

Stretch

1. Hold your index and middle finger on both hands like scissors.
2. Try to pick up an object, a pencil.
3. Pass the objects from one set of finger chopsticks to another
4. Put the object down.
5. Wiggle your fingers, all five on both hands.
6. Clench and unclench your fists.
7. Breathe.

Write

- Pick a food. Begin writing about it. Or a recipe. (Recipe/index cards can be used.)
- As you write, write in people you connect with this food.

Fitchness Tip

- Sometimes *real* writing take time; cooks slowly. Percolates. Other times, a feast can be whipped up in a jiffy.

I was teaching in a program at Arctic college called Dream Catchers. A student who had been quiet all week did the food exercise and shared. She wrote of her mother giving instructions for making bannock as she was dying of cancer. It was one of the most moving pieces I have ever read. Class stopped and, because our class had a kitchen and I had never tasted bannock, several of the women rustled around and found what they needed. In no time we were eating the bannock. We ate and talked about mothers and traditions, about sharing and love. About life and death.

Writing from experience about our own lives is a deep sharing. It takes courage and a willingness to be vulnerable. Like the Stretches, this should not be forced.

23. Eye Roll

So writing is about getting our voices and vision onto the page. This is about *your* vision—*your* way of seeing. This eye roll is a lot harder than it looks. It helps if you think of a clock. Go gentle. And see if you can see what you see in your mind's eye when you write.

Breathe

1. Always breathe in and out through your nose.
2. Place your hand close to but not on your belly, near your navel. Inhale. As you do, gently push your belly toward your hand.
3. Exhale. Pull your belly in. Imagine you navel touches your spine.
4. Do this three times.
5. Return to normal breathing.

Stretch

1. Sit, keeping your head facing front.
2. Inhale. Move your eyes slowly around the room clockwise.
3. Exhale. Close your eyes.
4. Open your eyes. Inhale and repeat in the opposite direction.

Write

1. EYES OPEN
   - Find a picture that moves you.
   - Describe it so someone else can picture it in his or her mind.

2. LOOK AGAIN
   - Fill in the blanks:

        as blue as _____
        as sharp as _____
        as dark as _____

   - Close your eyes. Breathe.
   - Open your eyes and look again.
   - Fill in the blanks with new images.

24. Just for the "L" of It

Writing requires concentration if we are to create a moment in a poem or story. We lift a moment up to the light and hold it out for the reader—for the reader to connect with or be grabbed by, captivated with. In this pose the energy flows both upward and outward. Feel the lines of energy and the floor beneath you; hold your back against an imaginary wall. Breathe and approach the writing as if you have all the room in the world to tell a complete and perfect story.

Breathe

1. Always breathe in and out through your nose.
2. Place your hand close to, but not on, your belly near your navel. Inhale. As you do, gently push your belly toward your hand.
3. Exhale. Pull your belly in. Imagine your navel touching your spine.
4. Do this three times.
5. Return to normal breathing.

Stretch

1. Sit comfortably with your legs outstretched straight in front.
2. Engage your thigh muscles and flex your feet. Your heels may come up off the floor.
3. Make your spine long.
4. Stack your shoulders directly on top of your hips.
5. Breathe and relax.

Write

1. POSTCARD STORY
   - Get an index card and pretend it is a postcard.
   - Use this opening line:

     "Who knew I'd end up here," she thought, as they put handcuffs on her.

   - You have five minutes or so to write the whole story—beginning, middle, end.

2. A-LITERATION
   - Write a paragraph choosing words so that there are many letter *L*'s as possible.
   - Read it aloud.

25. Butterfly

The soaring of imagination can be a beautiful and fragile thing. Catching our thoughts can be like trying to catch a butterfly in a net—a net with huge holes. Sit and drift and feel the difference between the slowness and then the hurried flurry. Think of how fleeting our ideas can be. Let one settle, hold on to the image or idea gently, and write.

Breathe

1. Always breathe in and out through your nose.
2. Place your hand close to, but not on, your belly near your navel. Inhale. As you do, gently push your belly toward your hand.
3. Exhale. Pull your belly in. Imagine your navel touching your spine.
4. Do this three times.
5. Return to normal breathing.

Stretch

1. Sit with the soles of your feet together.
2. Relax your knees and let them drop as close to the floor as possible.
3. Sit up tall and straight.
4. Gently and slowly, flap your legs as if they were wings.
5. Stop. Breathe. Repeat.

Write

1. BUTTERFLY COLORS
   - Pick a color. Write about it for five minutes.
   - When you can, find something for yourself in that color.

2. METAMORPHOSIS
Write a story about a moment in a life when something little happens and everything changes.

3. NOMAD
Write about someone who moves around from place to place in search of home.

4. CAUGHT!
Write as if you are a butterfly caught in a net.

5. ABOUT BUTTERFLIES
Research butterflies and write an unrhymed poem that includes five things you never knew about butterflies.

26. Tongue-Tied

This is play with words, and play with sound, and play with how we can find our way into sheer silliness and laughter. Play is a way of claiming your voice and experimenting with word choice.

Breathe

1. Always breathe in and out through your nose.
2. Place your hand close to, but not on, your belly near your navel. Inhale. As you do, gently push your belly toward your hand.
3. Exhale. Pull your belly in. Imagine your navel touching your spine.
4. Do this three times.
5. Return to normal breathing.

Stretch

1. Fold your tongue up inside your mouth.
2. Touch your upper palette with tip of your folded tongue.
3. Open your mouth and draw air in through it.
4. Exhale though both nostrils.
5. If you can, fold your tongue lengthwise like a straw. Draw in air through it.
6. Exhale through both nostrils.

Write

1. CAT GOT YOUR TONGUE
Write about a time you were so afraid or embarrassed you could not speak.

2. VOICES
Listen to voices all day. Write a piece called "Voices."

27. Be a Hero

Inspiration does not always come from a "eureka!" moment inside oneself and freezing the moment. Sometimes it comes from outside—from outside this time and place, or from others. Flood your thoughts with all the heroic people you can think of as you sit and breathe in their hero-ness. Now write like the hero you are.

Breathe

1. Always breathe in and out through your nose.
2. Place your hand close to, but not on, your belly near your navel. Inhale. As you do, gently push your belly toward your hand.
3. Exhale. Pull your belly in. Imagine your navel touching your spine.
4. Do this three times.
5. Return to normal breathing.

Stretch

1. Kneel on the floor (on a folded blanket to pad your knees, shins, and feet, if necessary), with your thighs perpendicular to the floor, and your inner knees together.
2. Slide your feet apart, slightly wider than your hips, tops of the feet flat on the floor.
3. Exhale and sit back halfway, with your torso leaning slightly forward. Sit down between your feet.
4. Lay your hands in your lap, one on the other, palms up. Or place them on your thighs, palms down.
5. Firm your shoulder blades against your back ribs and lift the top of your sternum. Lengthen your tailbone into the floor to anchor the back torso.
6. Breathe. Relax.
7. To come out, lift your buttocks slightly higher than the heels. Cross your ankles underneath your buttocks. Sit back over the feet and onto the floor.
8. Stretch your legs out in front of you. Bounce your knees up and down a few times on the floor. Wag from side to side.

Write

1. MY HERO
Pick a mentor in your life. Write for five minutes about that person.

2. A REAL HERO
Research your hero in history. Invite that person to your house. What does the hero do? Say?

3. SUPERHERO
Create your own superhero. Give your superhero a name and a costume; list their super powers. Make a comic strip.

28. Hair Pull/Neck Roll

The best way to understand how important this small stretch can be is to observe people next time you are out. How many times do you see people stretching their necks from side to side or reaching up to rub their shoulders? Go ahead roll and tug and rub and shrug. Scratch and breathe. Imagine your brain beneath your scalp getting a good invigorating workout.

Breathe

1. Always breathe in and out through your nose.
2. Place your hand close to, but not on, your belly near your navel. Inhale. As you do, gently push your belly toward your hand.
3. Exhale. Pull your belly in. Imagine your navel touching your spine.
4. Do this three times.
5. Return to normal breathing.

Stretch

1. Make your fingers into claws.
2. Tug the hair on your scalp—gently.
3. Roll your neck from left to right.
4. Repeat. Breathe.

Write

1. WEAR THIS HAT
   - Everyone gets a hat or is given an occupation: e.g., chef, nurse, construction worker
   - Pretend you are that person. Write in first-person narrative. This results in great monologues.

2. RHYMED METAPHORS
Can you write a rhymed metaphor? Some examples:

My brain is a clogged drain.
My mind is lemon rind.
Your eyes are chocolate surprise.

3. HEADACHES

- What's bugging you? Write it down, look at it carefully. Is there anything you can do to make it better?
- Make a list. Then rip it up or burn it.
- Write for five minutes a piece called "Acceptance."

Fitchness Tip
- The richest, most interesting details you need in order to write with truth and zest are usually right under your own roof. Or helmet.

A week of writing class with middle-school students at a summer camp in Cape Breton yielded some amazing results. One of the girls had worked hard all week and her efforts were "good." I knew, however, I hadn't found the exercise in which she could release or trust her true voice. This exercise did it. She put on a hardhat, the helmet of a construction worker, and wrote a monologue about how this guy felt on his lunch break: what he saw, how he thought. She completely captured his point of view, his diction, his character. It was both funny and sad. There he was, shooting the breeze, swinging his legs over the guardrail of a bridge, observing life with the profound truths of a philosopher. It was brilliant. For her, the freedom to be someone else helped her let go of self-consciousness, of what was right or wrong in her writing, and this released her authentic voice and a vision of the world. When I asked her how she was able to do this so convincingly, she laughed and said, "Easy—I've got five brothers."

29. Yawning Legs

"Open wide the doors of your perception," said poet William Blake. This is an opening exercise. Take it easy and slow. Opening up in writing takes time, too. Open up to wonder, to all you do not know in the world. Be curious!

Breathe

1. Always breathe in and out through your nose.
2. Place your hand close to, but not on, your belly near your navel. Inhale. As you do, gently push your belly toward your hand.
3. Exhale. Pull your belly in. Imagine your navel touching your spine.
4. Do this three times.
5. Return to normal breathing.

Stretch

1. Sit in a simple seated position.
2. Spread your legs apart as far as they can go.
3. Point your kneecaps to ceiling. Flex your feet.
4. Slowly and gently walk your hands forward between your legs.
5. Fold forward as far as possible with no pain. Move from your hips and keep lengthening the spine. Do not bend from the waist.
6. Breathe into the pose and release.

Write

1. FORTUNE COOKIE

You are fortune cookie writer. Write five fortunes and give them to whomever you wish.

2. FOLLOW THE STORY

Be an investigative reporter writing an article about whatever you choose. Write with the idea that what you uncover will make a difference in someone's life.

30. Fish Twist

A writer friend of mine once advised me: just when you think you've nailed the idea, turn it another few notches. I love to think of fish jumping in a river in this pose. They bend and seem to flex their muscles. For a brief moment, maybe they think they can fly. If fish can jump out of water, we can make a word splash—and take leaps of imagination.

Breathe

1. Always breathe in and out through your nose.
2. Place your hand close to, but not on, your belly near your navel. Inhale. As you do, gently push your belly toward your hand.
3. Exhale. Pull your belly in. Imagine your navel touching your spine.
4. Do this three times.
5. Return to normal breathing.

Stretch

1. Sit with legs straight in front of you.
2. Place your right foot over your left leg.
3. Bending your knees, slide your left foot under your right leg.
4. Point your right knee up.
5. Exhale and twist toward the inside of your right thigh.
6. Press your right hand against the floor behind your right buttock.
7. Set your left upper arm on the outside of right thigh near the knee.
8. Turn your head in direction of the twist.
9. Breathe; hold. Release.

Write

1. OPPOSITE
What is the opposite of fence? Write!

2. TWISTED THINGS
Write the same story from different points of view.

Fitchness Tip
- The creative writing prompt for Write #1 comes from a book called *The Pocket Muse* by Monica Woods. These books are filled with ideas and suggestions to spark creativity and refresh the writing process.

31. Funny Face

Let's face it. You've only got one face and that face is going to be with you for a long time. So you've got to learn to get along with that face you've got. Body language speaks volumes. We give off many clues through our facial expressions, and our faces can really speak louder than words—especially to someone who knows how to read the signals.

Breathe

1. Always breathe in and out through your nose.
2. Place your hand close to, but not on, your belly near your navel. Inhale. As you do, gently push your belly toward your hand.
3. Exhale. Pull your belly in. Imagine your navel touching your spine.
4. Do this three times.
5. Return to normal breathing.

Stretch

1. Sit in kneeling position, hands on thighs.
2. Slide your hands forward and let the your fingertips touch the floor.
3. Bend your body forward, buttocks off the heels, arms straight.
4. Open your eyes wide as possible.
5. Stick your tongue out far as it will go. Try to touch your chin.
6. Hold for fifteen seconds.
7. Repeat twice more.

Write

1. FILM SCRIPT OUTLINE
   - What movie would you make?
   - Give it a title. Write a synopsis. Decide who would star in it.

2. FACE IT
   - Look at your face in the mirror. Frown, smile, make a silly face.
   - All day, notice what people are doing with their faces. What are their faces telling you?
   - Write for five minutes a draft or beginning of free verse poem called "Real Face Books."

32. Camel

One lump or two? Sometimes we can get stuck in our habits, our thinking, and our writing. Writing is exhausting. This pose is challenging for many, restful to others. Do not push this pose. Just stay in kneeling position if that is most comfortable. Try not to compare yourself with others. If you must compare, compare with your own last best attempt—at writing or this pose!

Breathe

1. Always breathe in and out through your nose.
2. Place your hand close to, but not on, your belly near your navel. Inhale. As you do, gently push your belly toward your hand.
3. Exhale. Pull your belly in. Imagine your navel touching your spine.
4. Do this three times.
5. Return to normal breathing.

Stretch

1. Sit on your knees.
2. Reach behind your body and grab the soles of your feet if you can.
3. Breathe and hold.
4. Release.

Write

STUBBORN CAMEL

- Write a letter sounding off to your most challenging student/friend. Then rip it up.
- Write three words that you think are useful dealing with that challenging person.
- Write a piece called "Stick in the Mud."

The Reclining Exercises

At the end of every day, we go to bed and lie down. We take the weight of our bodies off our joints and the weight of our worries off our shoulders—if we can. We relax, breathe deeply, and prepare to sleep, perhaps to dream. We change the centre of gravity in our bodies. We enter the subconscious realm as we drift off to sleep.

Not all of these reclining poses are relaxing. But they do put more of the entire body in contact with the floor. We can get more in touch with our dreams and our creative selves in the poses that follow.

> *Each of us possesses a creative self. Claiming that is a transformational art. When you begin to act on your creativity, what you find inside may be more valuable than what you produce for the external world. The ultimate creative act is to express what is most authentic and individual about you.*
> —Eileen M. Clegg

33. Ssssnake

The image of a snake conjures up different emotions for different people—awe, wonder, fear. But snakes are powerful symbols of energy. They twist and turn. They have power in their poison and, for writers who have to begin again and again and again to jiggle words until they have a finished piece, the snake is a symbol of hope. Snakes shed skin to be new again. That is what we do each time we write. Shed the fear, find the new.

Breathe

1. Always breathe in and out through your nose.
2. Place your hand close to, but not on, your belly near your navel. Inhale. As you do, gently push your belly toward your hand.
3. Exhale. Pull your belly in. Imagine your navel touching your spine.
4. Do this three times.
5. Return to normal breathing.

Stretch

1. Lie on your belly, forehead on the ground, legs straight out behind you. Your hands are on the floor underneath your shoulders.
2. Inhale.
3. As you breathe out, push into the ground with your hands and elbows, and slowly raise your head and shoulders off the ground. Do not straighten your arms. Keep your elbows on the ground.
5. Inhale and lower your neck back down.
6. Exhale and try again.

Write

PERSONAL METAPHOR

- Write a personal metaphor. Here are some examples:

  I am a snake, slithering through the grass.
  I am a dot-to-dot puzzle. I still don't know what picture I'm trying to make.
  I am a turtle, slow and shy.
  I am a volcano, boiling with rage.

Here is one of my favorite personal metaphors from an older student:

> I am a nighthawk searching for food, shelter for me and my three children.

It was a true reflection of her life at that moment. Remember: pieces can be serious or funny!

Rattle Snake
in that
tree I
hope you
don't jump
out at
ME!
—*Carley, Grade 4 student*

---

34. Lift Bridge

Writing is making connections—from sentence to sentence, from page to page, from writer to reader. Words are stepping stones to form that bridge. Maybe you need to report on a disaster, create a story, or advertise something. The link to the reader? The words you use and choose, the order you use them in.

Breathe

1. Always breathe in and out through your nose.
2. Place your hand close to, but not on, your belly near your navel. Inhale. As you do, gently push your belly toward your hand.
3. Exhale. Pull your belly in. Imagine your navel touching your spine.
4. Do this three times.
5. Return to normal breathing.

Stretch

1. Lie on your back with your knees up and hands at your side. Your feet should be near your buttocks and about a hand-width apart.
2. Gently raise and lower your bottom. Then slowly raise your tailbone and continue lifting your spine, trying to move one vertebra at a time until your entire back is arched upward.
3. Push firmly down with your feet. Keep your knees straight and close together.
4. Breathe deeply into your chest.
5. Clasp your hands under your back and push against the floor.
6. Hold, taking slow, deep breaths.
7. Come down slowly and repeat.

Write

1. FLOOD
You are a reporter covering a flood. Write and share a piece on the flood.

2. BRIDGE TO NOWHERE
Write a story using the title "Bridge to Nowhere."

3. ATTENTION, ALL SHOPPERS!
- You work for a store. Write an advertisement for TV or radio.
- Make it wacky or serious! Convince me I have to have it. Include details: sights, sounds, colors, quantity, cost.

35. Rock the Boat

Writing can be all about rocking the boat, stirring things up, creating stories so people can see things in new and unexpected ways. There are many kinds of bodies of water: lake, river, stream, ocean. And many kinds of bodies. This is a pose that offers many possibilities.

Breathe

1. Always breathe in and out through your nose.
2. Place your hand close to, but not on, your belly near your navel. Inhale. As you do, gently push your belly toward your hand.
3. Exhale. Pull your belly in. Imagine your navel touching your spine.
4. Do this three times.
5. Return to normal breathing.

Stretch

1. Lie on your back. Visualize the mat around your body as a body of water.
2. Sit up in L position (see page 57).
3. Bring your knees toward your chest.
4. Extend your legs at a 45 degree angle, making a V with your body. Keep your knees bent if straightening them is too difficult.
5. Bring your arms out straight forward from the shoulders.
6. Gently rock back and forth.

Write

1. INVITATION
   - Write an invitation to someone you have never met, having them come with you on a voyage by boat.
   - What would you say so they would love to come? Remember senses and specifics. No need to research—just imagine.

2. DOWN WITH THE SHIP
Research a shipwreck. Write an unrhymed poem about it.

3. WAVES
Write a poem in lines that move like waves.

36. Child Pose

What does it mean to be a child? Wonder. Awe. Vulnerability. Relief. Openness. This is my favorite pose. For me it is a once-a-day stretch. And I wish every child in every class had a chance to be a child like this every day. Or maybe once a week? Child pose returns us to almost the complete beginning. Here I am. Ready or not.

Breathe

1. Always breathe in and out through your nose.
2. Place your hand close to, but not on, your belly near your navel. Inhale. As you do, gently push your belly toward your hand.
3. Exhale. Pull your belly in. Imagine your navel touching your spine.
4. Do this three times.
5. Return to normal breathing.

Stretch

1. Kneel with your legs together.
2. Rest your buttocks on your heels and the top of your hands on the floor pointing back.
3. Lower your head slowly to the floor, hands sliding back, palms up, to lie beside the body.
4. Rest your head, turned to the side, on the floor. Relax completely with your chest against the knees.
5. Hold for any length of time, but not long enough to fall asleep.

VARIATION
- Stretch your arms out beyond your head, with your elbows by your ears.

Write

1. FILL-IN-THE-BLANK SIMILES
- Teacher says prompt and everyone fills in the answer individually. Go down the list very quickly at first. Give time, but not too much time.
- Here are some prompts: As red as…; As dark as…; As cold as…; As blue as…; As hard as…; As soft as…; As slippery as…; As hot as…; As sour as…; As sweet as …; As stinky as…
- When done, find out what everyone wrote. See how many had "As dark as night." Or "As blue as the sky." Go back to list and replace something lame or cliché with something surprising.

When forced to do writing too fast, sometimes we fall back on first idea, the cliché. It does take time to get to an original way of seeing, so remember that there are many kinds of red, or soft, or anything. I love to give the example of an eight-year-old boy who once wrote "As dark as night" first go round. When I asked him to come up with the darkest dark he could think of he wrote, "As dark as the mouth of a killer whale," then he used it next day in a story.

A memorable moment: "As stinky as my grama's house" one eight-year-old wrote and read loud. All his classmates started laughing. I was momentarily lost for words. "Well, she raises pigs you know," he said defensively. "PERFECT simile!" I said, to which he beamed, and the others stopped laughing.

2. IMAGE EXERCISE
- Come up with some emotion words; e.g., Loneliness, Happiness, Beauty.
- Make them visual by painting a concrete image with words:

> Loneliness—a phone that never rings.
> Happiness—a freezie on a hot day.
> Beauty—a finished Kamik.

Almost fifteen years ago, I offered the above exercise to a group of Grade 5 students. When I asked if anyone wanted to share one girl put up her hands. She read:

> Loneliness
> Sitting a chair
> outside the courtroom
> the day your parents
> get divorced.

Fitchness Tip
- Approaching writing to explore process so that we get to authentic writing is not a therapy session. But do not be surprised at how emotional a class can become.
- Learning happens in the unexpected turns and twists, the detours you make in a writing class, a road that leads you to discover new landscapes and enjoy a view you may not have known was even there.

I gulped. Swallowed. "You made Sheree Fitch cry!" I heard a shocked whisper. "Yes," I said quickly, "but that is because she wrote the loneliest lonely I have ever read. Good writing can make a person cry, and tears are okay. They are. Truth is powerful." Our class went on that day in what I can only say is the tenderest of ways. A few moments later one of the boys wrote of his best friend who had died from cancer the year before. "He lives among a bed of rocks," was his first line. Their teacher told me later that class had suffered greatly from the loss of their classmate and that boy had never spoken of the loss of his friend until that day. I learned so much that day. I learned how children know deep pain; how sharing stories is a deep way of connecting and healing.

37. Play Dead

Feel your whole body flop on the floor like a ragdoll with no spine, the stuffing all gone. Become as still as you can. Think of being outside your body and seeing your body below you. This is how a writer sometimes has to look at a scene or a story, as an outside observer. Relax every muscle. Make sure your jaw is loose and open. Can you be still if you are anxious or wanting it to be over? Shh. Try to almost go to sleep. What dream are you dreaming?

Breathe

1. Always breathe in and out through your nose.
2. Place your hand close to, but not on, your belly near your navel. Inhale. As you do, gently push your belly toward your hand.
3. Exhale. Pull your belly in. Imagine your navel touching your spine.
4. Do this three times.
5. Return to normal breathing.

Stretch

1. Lie on your back. Flop your feet out hip-width apart.
2. Close your eyes. Connect your body with the ground from your head to your toes. Imagine yourself sinking into the floor.
3. Concentrate on the darkness behind your eyelids. Breathe deeply, aware of each inhalation and exhalation.
4. When ready, come out of pose. Wiggle your toes and fingers.
5. Curl into fetal position. Rest your hand on the mat and push up slowly.
6. Open eyes. Maintain quiet.

Write

1. A DREAM
Recall a dream. Write for five minutes.

2. GHOST
Write a scene from the point of view of a ghost.

3. PARAMEDIC
Write an ambulance scene from the point of view of a paramedic.

38. Happy Baby

Babies stick their toes in the air—and in their mouths and in their noses. Squeal—say, "Goo goo!"

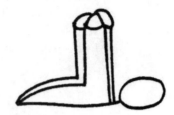

Breathe

1. Always breathe in and out through your nose.
2. Place your hand close to, but not on, your belly near your navel. Inhale. As you do, gently push your belly toward your hand.
3. Exhale. Pull your belly in. Imagine your navel touching your spine.
4. Do this three times.
5. Return to normal breathing.

Stretch

1. Lie on your back.
2. Bring your knees to your belly.
3. Grip the outside of your feet with each hand.
4. Open your knees and bring them towards your armpits. Keep your arms inside your legs as you raise them.
5. Flex your feet.
6. Hold and release.

Write

1. LULLABY

Write a love poem lullaby to anyone—even an animal. It can be unrhymed or rhymed.

2. HAPPY PERSON
- Write about peaceful person. What soothes this person? How does this character relax? What is this character's name? Where does this person live? CREATE!
- Now write what makes you peaceful.
- Variation: Cranky Baby! Write a list of things that make you angry. Create an angry character. What has hurt this person? What is this character afraid of?

3. KIDS BOOK
- Come up with an idea for kids book in five minutes.
- Brainstorm ideas with a partner.
- Suggested follow-up: Write a picture book. Storyboard the art.

39. Cat and Dog

This pose gives a good sense of opposites: arch and curve; concave and convex. In every story there needs to be something at stake for the main character—a goal or desire—and something working against the character achieving that goal or desire. We call this the dramatic tension of a story. Can you feel the tension in your body shift as you do these poses? Experiment with rhythm: rock back and forth—slower, faster. There is a pace in every story. The author is in control.

Breathe

1. Always breathe in and out through your nose.
2. Place your hand close to, but not on, your belly near your navel. Inhale. As you do, gently push your belly toward your hand.
3. Exhale. Pull your belly in. Imagine your navel touching your spine.
4. Do this three times.
5. Return to normal breathing.

Stretch

1. Lie on your stomach.
2. Raise yourself on your hands and knees until you are on all fours.
2. Inhale, pressing your navel to your spine (Cat).
3. Exhale. Let your belly sink (Dog).
4. Repeat from dog to cat several times.

Write

1. MOVING DOGS AND CATS

Write a piece about a character with a dog and a cat who wants to get to another place. What are the problems? How are they solved?

2. CAT RULES/DOG RULES

Write ten sayings you think are good rules to live by if you were a dog or a cat.

I once had a beagle dog. His name was Babes. One morning as I was making breakfast I dropped a bagel on the floor. Babes started eating the bagel. I thought, "Oh, a beagle eating a bagel," and my poet brain went to work. *Beagle, Bagel. Beagle, Bagel. I should put that together in a poem some day.* I scribbled the lines down. I wrote and wrote and nothing happened. So I saved it for another day. A few months later I was in British Columbia during a break while doing readings in a library. I took a look around. There was a wonderful poster of a beluga whale. I stood there in the library thinking how beautiful the beluga whale was. I stood there thinking how beautiful the word *beluga* was. *Beluga, beluga,* I said to myself. *That beluga belongs with the beagle and the bagel.* And I stored that idea away. And I wrote and I wrote and nothing happened. And many years after that I was asked to write a book for UNICEF on the United Nations Convention on the Rights of the Child. I decided I wanted to finish that beagle bagel beluga poem, and I did. Here it is:

Fitchness Tip

- Don't try to rush a finished piece. See how long it took for this one to go from first burst to finished poem?

The Boogie Woogie Beagle Beluga Blues
There was a beagle
Who loved bagels

In fact he loved to beg for bagels
Wagged his tail for bagels
Whenever bugles blew
One day the beagle met a beluga
Who played the boogie woogie bugle

The beagle giggled: "Hi Beluga!"
Then played a jig with his kazoo.

Then the beagle and the beluga
Eating bagels, blowing bugles
Met a eagle who was eager
To eat some buttered bagels too

So...
The eagle and the beagle and the bugle-playing beluga sailed together

Saw the
    seven
        million
            wonders
                of the world !!!!
Such a boondoggling
    Mindboggling
        Hornswoggling time !

It was the boogie woogie eager eagle beagle beluga blues!

40. Up Back Over Your Head

This is a great pose for those who are flexible enough to get their feet up and over their head. As in every pose, slow is often better and less is more. No pain. No strain. So it can be with writing, when you are in the zone, letting it flow. But you still have to take time in revision if you want to offer your writing for someone to read in print. In this pose it is essential that your shoulders stay firm against the mat. Picture an upside-down letter V. Keep enough room between your knees and your chest so that you can breathe. Keep enough distance between your first burst of writing and your next draft so that the ideas have time to breathe.

Breathe

1. Always breathe in and out through your nose.
2. Place your hand close to, but not on, your belly near your navel. Inhale. As you do, gently push your belly toward your hand.
3. Exhale. Pull your belly in. Imagine your navel touching your spine.
4. Do this three times.
5. Return to normal breathing.

Stretch

1. Lie on your back.
2. Lift your legs, pushing your hands down on floor.
3. Slowly bring your legs over your head, keeping them straight. Try to touch your feet to the floor.
5. Hold if comfortable. Breathe.
6. Slowly come out of pose.

Write

1. I AM...
   - Fill in the blank: *I Am....*
   - Put together everyone's personal metaphors and end on positive one, like *I am an eagle.*

2. THE SPACE
   - Write for 15 minutes around the title "The Space."
   - Wait a week. Then go back to rework the piece.

41. Rock and Roll

Make sure you have a mat underneath you. Rock 'n' roll! At the best of times, writing is kind of word music. Find a beat with your body. Experiment. Feel your backbones like a zipper; zip yourself up and then down. Feel your blood surging. At the best of times, writing feels like a rock and a roll of syllables, sentences, paragraphs. Words!

Breathe

1. Always breathe in and out through your nose.
2. Place your hand close to, but not on, your belly near your navel. Inhale. As you do, gently push your belly toward your hand.
3. Exhale. Pull your belly in. Imagine your navel touching your spine.
4. Do this three times.
5. Return to normal breathing.

Stretch

1. Lie on your back.
2. Bend your knees to your chest.
3. Clasp hands around your knees, hugging your legs to your chest.
4. Rock back and forth. Start slowly, then you can rock with more force.
5. Play with the speed of your rocking.
6. Stop; breathe; release legs to floor.

Write

1. TEN COMMANDMENTS
Write your personal creed or ten commandments that apply to your life now.

2. THE MALL
- Write as if you were an old person waiting to go to the mall.
- Write about the character going to the mall from another point of view.

42. The Bow

If you are the bow, your words are the arrows that can pierce the reader's heart, and maybe get through into his or her head. Think of words and how precisely we use them as you execute this pose. Think of the sharpness of images and the edges of characters. Think of the intent you have in writing. What do you care about? What do you want your reader to know? How will you get this across?

Breathe

1. Always breathe in and out through your nose.
2. Place your hand close to, but not on, your belly near your navel. Inhale. As you do, gently push your belly toward your hand.
3. Exhale. Pull your belly in. Imagine your navel touching your spine.
4. Do this three times.
5. Return to normal breathing.

Stretch

1. Lie on your belly, hands alongside your body.
2. Exhale and bend your knees, bringing heels as close to your buttocks as you can.
3. Reach back with your hands and grab your ankles.
4. Inhale, lifting your heels away from your buttocks and your thighs off the floor.
5. Press your shoulder blades together to open up your chest.
6. Keep breathing. Release.

Write

ACROSTIC POEM

Write an unrhymed acrostic poem using the first letters of TEACHER, or a word of your choosing:

T
E
A
C
H
E
R

43. Push Up

Push yourself. Don't push! Push through. Push out. We get pushed around. We push doors open and push ideas around. The verb "push" is a pushy word. Push open doors to your ideas. Push against fear and ordinary ways of thinking.

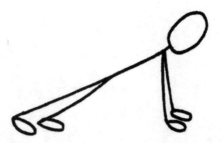

Breathe

1. Always breathe in and out through your nose.
2. Place your hand close to, but not on, your belly near your navel. Inhale. As you do, gently push your belly toward your hand.
3. Exhale. Pull your belly in. Imagine your navel touching your spine.
4. Do this three times.
5. Return to normal breathing.

Stretch

1. Start in Downward Dog pose (see page 42).
2. Draw your body forward until your arms are perpendicular to the floor and you are in push-up position.
3. Hold.
4. Breathe; release.

Write

1. DO IT YOURSELF

Write a how-to of something you know how to do well for someone who does not know. It can be serious or silly.

2. LIFT

Describe lifting an object that is heavy; one that is light; one that is awkward to lift; one that is invisible.

44. Dolphin

From breath, to length, to strength. In a completed piece or writing, we use words to shape meaning. Experiment with breath in this pose. Be aware. Hold the pose for as long as you can. Release. Write for as long as you can. Stop.

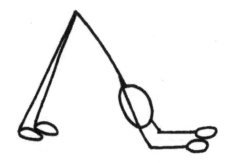

Breathe

1. Always breathe in and out through your nose.
2. Place your hand close to, but not on, your belly near your navel. Inhale. As you do, gently push your belly toward your hand.
3. Exhale. Pull your belly in. Imagine your navel touching your spine.
4. Do this three times.
5. Return to normal breathing.

Stretch

1. Lie on your stomach. Lift yourself on your hands and knees to get on all fours.
2. Place your forearms on the floor, with your shoulders above your wrists.
3. Press your palms together
4. Curl your toes under. Exhale, lifting knees.
5. Lift your sitting bones toward the ceiling.
6. Firm your shoulder blades; widen, then rotate them down toward tailbone.
7. Hold your head between your arms. Do not let it dangle.
8. Hold; breathe; release.

Write

1. UNDERWATER

Write an underwater scene. Describe it from a diver's point of view. Then write from a dolphin's point of view.

2. ON SET

Write about a favorite place—indoors or out—as if it were a movie location.

The Moving Exercises

Stand up, sit down, lie down...now get moving!

When you start to move, your circulation will improve—not just blood circulation. The ideas and thoughts that swirl and spin will circulate and flow in new ways as we connect more and more with body and breath. We can get "unstuck" from any old tired and rigid ways of thinking and perceiving. We can make space, move into new and unfamiliar positions, and marvel at how the territory and landscape of our imagination shifts and expands. It's amazing how, when we begin from a place of stillness and start to move around, we discover how we move on, move ahead.

Happiness consists in activity. It is a running stream, not a stagnant pool.
—John Mason Good

45. The Twist

When I was a kid, this was the dance to do. It is great for abdominals and for working up a sweat in no time. But you can easily get a stitch in your side from twisting too vigorously, so watch it.

Breathe
1. Always breathe in and out through your nose.
2. Place your hand close to, but not on, your belly near your navel. Inhale. As you do, gently push your belly toward your hand.
3. Exhale. Pull your belly in. Imagine your navel touching your spine.
4. Do this three times.
5. Return to normal breathing.

Stretch
1. Stand.
2. Do the old-fashioned dance the Twist. (Music makes it more fun!)
3. Crouch down, stand up, all while twisting. Get your heart beating faster.
4. Then slow down the twist, and return to seated position.
5. Breathe normally.

Write

1. STARTS WITH...
   - Choose a letter of the alphabet, avoiding *X*.
   - Teacher prompts, "On your mark; get set; go."
   - Start writing words that begin with that letter.
   - Teacher stops the writing after about a minute and asks everyone to read their lists aloud at the same time. It will be a mumble jumble.
   - Teacher asks one person to read his or her list alone. Then again a little louder. It will sound like a tongue twister.

This is good chance to talk about the music of words. No, it does not have to make sense. This exercise is excellent to break through fear, a good one to return to again and again. A riot. A romp! Very often an invented word will make its way into the list—*dog, daily, dead, dang, deed, dollars, drutters, dear*! Drutters. Hmm. *Drutters.* Maybe that is when a dragon mutters. Drutters. Perfect. Yes, I used it in a book. Never overlook your mistakes!

2. TWIST OF THE TALE

Write a mini mystery. First, write from the point of view of the bad guy or gal. Then switch to writing as the good guy or gal.

> *Creativity is 1 percent inspiration and 99 percent perspiration.*
> —Thomas Edison

> *Think left and think right and think low and think high. Oh, the thinks you can think up if only you try!*
> —Dr. Seuss

46. Go Crazy!

Writing is a dance of words. A poem is a dance of syllables. Let your bodies dance and your pen dance. And have fun!

Breathe

1. Always breathe in and out through your nose.
2. Place your hand close to, but not on, your belly near your navel. Inhale. As you do, gently push your belly toward your hand.
3. Exhale. Pull your belly in. Imagine your navel touching your spine.
4. Do this three times.
5. Return to normal breathing.

Stretch

1. Stand in Stand on Your Own Two Feet pose (see page 22).
2. Straighten and stiffen body
3. Relax.
4. Shake every part of your body.
5. Shout, "Do the Shaky Shaky Thing!" if you like.
6. Stop. Breathe.

Write

1. DANCING TREES
Write a piece with the title "Dancing Trees."

2. TONGUE TWISTER
Write a tongue twister with the words "shimmy," "shake," and "shiver" in it.

47. Bowing/Curtsying

This is harder than it looks! In some cultures, it is a sign of great respect to bow when you meet someone. With this exercise we can practice cultivating and nurturing respect for our own bodies and each other. We can show respect and appreciation for the blank page and our chance to write words and speak some truths.

Breathe

1. Always breathe in and out through your nose.
2. Place your hand close to, but not on, your belly near your navel. Inhale. As you do, gently push your belly toward your hand.
3. Exhale. Pull your belly in. Imagine your navel touching your spine.
4. Do this three times.
5. Return to normal breathing.

Stretch

1. Stand in Stand on Your Own Two Feet pose (see page 22).
2. Bend forward at the waist. (Bow)
3. Come back up to standing pose.
4. Cross your legs at the ankles. Dip knees out the side. (Curtsy)
5. Return to standing position.

Write

1. THANK YOU, MEMBERS OF THE ACADEMY
Write a speech on winning an award. Include details of what you did to win it, and what kind of award it is.

2. LOVE LETTER
Write a love letter to yourself. Go ahead—brag, brag, brag! This can be the hardest exercise ever.

3. HOW TO...
- Write how to be a person, from the point of view of a dog who has deeply observed humans.
- Write a piece called "Manners: The Ten Most Important Manners for Everyone."

4. YOUR MAJESTY
Write a story about the day you (or a character) met a Queen or King.

48. Hand-to Toe-Balancing Act

Life is an everyday process of finding our balance. In the stories of our own lives, teachers are often juggling work and play, family obligations and our need for time for ourselves. We are often weighing things and making decisions. Our hearts do not always make logical sense, and using only our heads can distance us from empathy and the compassion we need for ourselves so we can extend it to each other. To write and to live, keep working and playing at finding balance. Begin with stillness and breath. Then write to discover/uncover how many things everyone is trying to keep juggling all at once.

Breathe

1. Always breathe in and out through your nose.
2. Place your hand close to, but not on, your belly near your navel. Inhale. As you do, gently push your belly toward your hand.
3. Exhale. Pull your belly in. Imagine your navel touching your spine.
4. Do this three times.
5. Return to normal breathing.

Stretch

1. Start in Stand on Your Own Two Feet pose (see page 22). Focus on spot in front of you.
2. Bend your left leg, grasp the big toe with your left hand; hold and breathe.
3. Exhale, extending right arm for balance. Straighten your left leg as far as you can.
4. Experiment with moving your left leg from side to front.
5. Come back to centre. Release.
6. Repeat on opposite side.

Write

1. **HEADLINES**
   - Find the first magazine you can and read the cover headlines.
   - Headline your life at the moment. Be as funny or serious as you want.

2. **THE BALANCING ACT**
Write a short skit called "The Balancing Act." Name each cast member with a name that describes that person's personality; e.g., Bubbles, Earnest, Mr. Grumble.

3. **ACTING OUT**
Create a chaotic situation. Act it out.

49. Jumping Jacks

This exercise is vigorous and energetic. Explore slow-motion jumping jacks; try small-motion and large-motion. In our writing, verbs are action words and say more than any adjective ever will to a reader or listener. Jump into the world of words and start collecting verbs like they are nuggets of gold.

Breathe

1. Always breathe in and out through your nose.
2. Place your hand close to, but not on, your belly near your navel. Inhale. As you do, gently push your belly toward your hand.
3. Exhale. Pull your belly in. Imagine your navel touching your spine.
4. Do this three times.
5. Return to normal breathing.

Stretch

1. Stand in Stand on Your Own Two Feet pose (see page 22).
2. Raise arms to both sides and overhead in one motion, jumping your legs apart as you do.
3. Lower your arms back to your sides, jumping your feet back together.
4. Repeat and execute with vigor a few times.
5. Return to standing pose.
6. Wait until heart is calm and breath is steady.

Write

1. OPPOSITES
   - All day, be aware of opposites—up, down; happy, sad; black, white; etc.
   - Write for five minutes on the title "Contradictions in Life."
   - Write for five minutes on the title "Balancing Act."

2. COLLECTING VERBS
   - Pick a verb or two or three
   - Get a thesaurus. Write down synonyms you find for that verb.
   - Create sentences using the verbs. What happens?

50. Shoulder Shrugs

The shoulder shrug is easy to do on the spot in a chair. Keep your back straight and upper diaphragm lifted; keep you chest out. Then, execute the pose. Try to touch your shoulders to your earlobes. A shrug communicates the idea of "I don't know." This exercise can be a way of having fun with the phrase. As we lift and release the shoulders, repeat, "I don't know… I don't know."

Breathe

1. Always breathe in and out through your nose.
2. Place your hand close to, but not on, your belly near your navel. Inhale. As you do, gently push your belly toward your hand.
3. Exhale. Pull your belly in. Imagine your navel touching your spine.
4. Do this three times.
5. Return to normal breathing.

Stretch

1. Stand in Stand on Your Own Two Feet pose (see page 22) or sit in a simple seated pose (see page 46).
2. Inhale, raising shoulders to earlobes.
3. Exhale, lowering your shoulders.
4. Inhale and repeat the shrug, this time rounding the shoulders backward.
5. Exhale, lowering your shoulders.

Write

1. WHAT I DON'T KNOW
Write a list of things you don't know, but want to know about.

2. CREATE A CHARACTER
Invent a name and a job for a character. Start writing using that character.

51. Bear Walk

Touch the earth with your hands and knees; embody the bulk and spirit of the Bear—it can be very powerful. Growl and breathe. Feel the muscles in your back stretch and the energy move through your neck. Feel the entire release from deep in your throat. Be fierce...or funny. Are you ready to hibernate or to protect your cubs? How do you rear up on your hind legs? Experiment and be any four-legged animal you want—feel the shift in energy as you try to inhabit the essence of a coyote, or zebra, or warthog.

Breathe

1. Always breathe in and out through your nose.
2. Place your hand close to, but not on, your belly near your navel. Inhale. As you do, gently push your belly toward your hand.
3. Exhale. Pull your belly in. Imagine your navel touching your spine.
4. Do this three times.
5. Return to normal breathing.

Stretch

1. Get down on all fours.
2. Begin crawling and growling.
3. Keeping distance from others, growl in their direction.
4. Crawl backward. Crawl into a "cave," real (under a table) or imaginary.
5. Relax on your back, feet and hands in the air. Continue roaring.
6. Hibernate. Snore.

Write

1. FAIRY TALE

Remember a favorite story from a fairy tale, like Goldilocks and the Three Bears. Imagine you are in a coffee shop with a character from that story. What would you say to each other?

I was once having lunch with a children's librarian, when in walked a woman who looked exactly like a character from one of my favorite books of all time— Miss Rumphius by Barbara Cooney. "Look!" I said to Linda, my librarian friend. "When you can, look over your left shoulder at the woman seated at the table. Who does that woman remind you of?" She looked as discreetly as possible. "Miss Rumphius," she replied. Exactly! Those stories and characters we love sometimes have a way of coming to life.

2. MY BEAR CAVE
Write about where you would go to hibernate.

3. DARE TO BE
Research animals from a particular place; e.g., the savannah in Africa. Find out how they live and what their relationships are with other animals. Do you dare write from a hyena's point of view?

Life is like riding a bicycle. To keep your balance you must keep moving.
—Albert Einstein

We don't stop playing because we grow old; we grow old because we stop playing.
—George Bernard Shaw

52. Funny Walks

Walk, walk, walk. Walk until you laugh. The aim of this exercise is to get laughing. Walk, waddle, rock…and laugh.

Breathe

1. Always breathe in and out through your nose.
2. Place your hand close to, but not on, your belly near your navel. Inhale. As you do, gently push your belly toward your hand.
3. Exhale. Pull your belly in. Imagine your navel touching your spine.
4. Do this three times.
5. Return to normal breathing.

Stretch

1. Stand in Stand on Your Own Two Feet pose (see page 22).
2. Exhale with a little "Ha!"
3. Begin penquin-walking. Giggle if you feel like it.
4. Stop and walk like a monkey, making monkey laughter sounds.
5. Hop and laugh as if you were at a funny movie.
6. Keep laughing, making funny faces at others.
7. Stop; connect with breath; return to normal breathing.

Write

1. WALKING THE WALK
   - Write a story from a penguin's point of view.
   - Write comparing monkeys with something out of control in your life.

2. FUNNY SONG
Write a stanza to begin a corny love song.

> *Laughter Yoga combines laughter with yogic breathing exercises. It is a perfect way to laugh and get exercise at the same time. It approaches laughter as a body exercise so it's easy to laugh even if you're depressed or in a bad mood. I've tried it, and it works.*
> —Oprah Winfrey

53. Months of the Year or Sun Salutation

With this sequence of stretches, the more you practice, the more the poses become natural and a part of you. Repeating the month of year helps the process. Soon, this will become something you can do without thinking or remembering. Your body has memory and will start moving into each phase automatically; as you feel the flow your body will just go there. When we write without thinking or grasping and just let the words flow, story comes naturally. We write deeply, authentically.

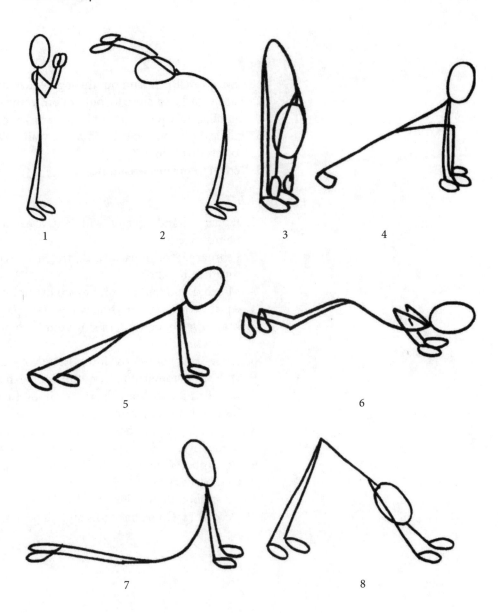

1   2   3   4

5   6

7   8

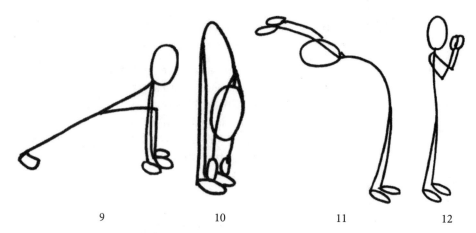

9   10   11   12

Breathe

1. Always breathe in and out through your nose.
2. Place your hand close to, but not on, your belly near your navel. Inhale. As you do, gently push your belly toward your hand.
3. Exhale. Pull your belly in. Imagine your navel touching your spine.
4. Do this three times.
5. Return to normal breathing.

Stretch

1. January: Stand straight, with your arms bent at the elbows and your palms together.
2. February: Stretch backward; stretch arms over head with hands still together, inhaling.
3. March: Bend forward and touch the floor, exhaling.
4. April: Strike a Runners Start pose (see page 40), inhaling.
5. May: Stretch forward, raising your body while resting on your hands. Retain breath.
6. June: Bring your body down. Raise your elbows and rest on your hands, with your stomach up from the floor, exhaling.
7. July: Bring your body flat on the floor. Raise your shoulders and chest. Rest on hands, inhaling.
8. August: Slide your hands back, raising your buttocks up so your body is in the inverted V shape of Downward Dog (see page 42).
9. September: Come back to Runners Start pose (see page 40).
10. October: Repeat step 3.
11. November: Repeat step 2.
12. December: Come back to standing pose with palms together at heart.

Write

1. RESOLUTIONS

Pick a person you are having some "weirdnesses" with. Imagine you are alone with that person somewhere safe but private. Write a five-minute dialogue of what that person would say to you. What happens? Now reverse. Speak back.

2. CYCLES

Write about some kind of cycle: e.g., the change of seasons; the passing of life; the routine of every day. A unicycle. A bicycle. A cyclone.

3. SUN SALUTATION

Think of all the things the sun does and means to people. Write a love poem to the sun.

If no other pose is learned, the sun salutation can be a friend for life. Sometimes just once through the sequence can start the day off right, close the day, or begin a writing session. When it's done a few times, the blood really flows. Holding the downward dog position and breathing into that pose for five breaths will calm, relax, restore the mind.

> *Take care of your body with steadfast fidelity. The soul must see through these eyes alone, and if they are dim, the whole world is clouded.*
> —Goethe

Group Moves

Writing is a solitary journey most of the time—unless we set out to collaborate. There are times, however, when two heads are better than one. And any time activity can be shared, the combination of energy can result in new and exciting ways of thinking and playing.

These are just a few suggestions for exercises for two or more people. Invent your own group huddles and then write—and see what ideas blossom forth. Sometimes working together takes the pressure of being in the spotlight off those who have no desire to be there; they find safety in numbers. Often, the thoughts and feelings of a group are brought closer together by the members physically being closer together. This proximity can create a safe place from which each individual can relax and feel empowered enough to share their words.

> *I tell you and you forget, I show you and you remember, I involve you and you understand.*
> —Confucius

54. Partner Breathing

This pose works best if people of roughly the same height are paired together. Just being aware of another's body, of touching someone, can be strange and unfamiliar for some. Being respectful and gentle with each other is one way to realize we can get in sync with each other. Breathing together makes us aware of the beating of each other's hearts, and reminds us of the fragility of everyone.

Breathe

1. Always breathe in and out through your nose.
2. Place your hand close to, but not on, your belly near your navel. Inhale. As you do, gently push your belly toward your hand.
3. Exhale. Pull your belly in. Imagine your navel touching your spine.
4. Do this three times.
5. Return to normal breathing.

Stretch

1. Get in pairs.
2. Stand back-to-back with your partner.
3. Inhaling, raise your arms to the sides and take hold of your partner's hands.
4. As you exhale slowly, lift your arms over the head to where it is comfortable.
5. As you inhale slowly, bring your arms back together at your sides.
6. Sit down in a simple seated pose (see page 46).

Write

1. FAVORITE FUNNY STORY
   - Tell your partner the funniest story you can think of. You have five minutes to both tell your stories.
   - Come back to the group. Tell your partner's story to the group.

2. SPOONERIZE YOUR NAME
   - Quick! Inhale and, as you exhale, create a spoonerism of your name (see page 31).
   - Write one whole sentence just lipslipping along: e.g., By mest whiend, Feather Hish, fistles wheally rell. (*My best friend Heather Fish, whistles really well.*)

55. London Bridge

A bridge is a structure that arches over a body of water and makes a link between two places. Without bridges, we can get from one point to the next only traveling by boat. This is why we write—to connect, to link. Think of the words we write as a bridge between us and the readers. Where are we going? What do we want to connect?

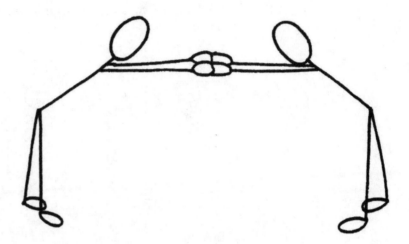

Breathe

1. Always breathe in and out through your nose.
2. Place your hand close to, but not on, your belly near your navel. Inhale. As you do, gently push your belly toward your hand.
3. Exhale. Pull your belly in. Imagine your navel touching your spine.
4. Do this three times.
5. Return to normal breathing.

Stretch

1. Stand facing your partner.
2. Grasp your partner's hands. Back away from each other a step or two.
3. Exhaling, bend at the hips toward your partner.
4. Take little steps back until your arms and back are in a straight line. Keep your legs straight and your heels on the floor.
5. Inhaling, stretch your sit bones back away from your partner.
6. Exhale and inhale. Feel your shoulder blades opening up.
7. When you're ready to release, step toward your partner, release your hands, and slowly roll up to standing position again.

Write

WORD GIVERS

- Write a word on a piece of paper and fold it up.
- Trade words with others by passing your paper to the left, or putting the words in a circle and everyone choosing one.
- Open the paper, look at the word. Without thinking too much, write for five minutes on that word.
- Read and share.

Fitchness Tip
- This is a great exercise to do many times. It's amazing what can emerge.

56. Body Sculpture

There really is a kind of safety in numbers. This is a free-flowing activity because everyone is up and loose and in a state of anticipation—there's no right or wrong. We know we are in process and the result is not under our control. It's an exploration, a creation, a collaboration, a mystery. In these ways, it is like every piece of deep and authentic writing. Starting with a word, a feeling is triggered. If one person takes the stance to begin, others will lose self-consciousness and follow. So shout out your theme: Inspiration! Vacation! Or homework! And ask everyone to just go!

Breathe

1. Always breathe in and out through your nose.
2. Place your hand close to, but not on, your belly near your navel. Inhale. As you do, gently push your belly toward your hand.
3. Exhale. Pull your belly in. Imagine your navel touching your spine.
4. Do this three times.
5. Return to normal breathing.

Stretch

1. Gather together in the group. Pick a theme: an emotion, activity, or concept; e.g., Happiness, Hurt, Healing, Sadness, etc. Shout out the word.
2. Make two groups. Assign someone in Group 1 to begin by striking a pose.
3. Build on that pose by having everyone in Group 1 in turn add on to the pose when they are inspired. Sculptors can use hand, foot, or shoulder contact. Group 2 observes.
4. When the sculpture is done, hold it for a moment. Take a photo if you can.
5. Switch groups so Group 2 builds the sculpture and Group 1 observes.

Write

1. GROUP POEM
   - For five minutes everyone writes.
   - Each group shares writing within the group.
   - Groups present to each other.

2. A LINE APIECE
   - The group chooses one line from each person to create a group poem.
   - Groups present to each other.

3. TOGETHER

As individuals, write a piece called "Togetherness Can Change the World."

Fitchness Tip
- Specifics!
- Senses!
- Clarity!
- Truth!

After Words

This book was inspired by the students and teachers who have been in my workshops. They have taught me so many things:

- There is no right or wrong way to encourage the creative writer.
- Everyone has stories buried deep inside.
- Writing takes courage and confidence and practice.
- Excellence is something we learn by reading and asking why some of what we read is powerful.

My writing journey continues, and I hope yours will too.

Teachers, writers, teachers who write—if you have found this book helpful in working with your students, tell me your *Breathe, Stretch, Write* stories. Go to my website at shereefitch.com and send me e-mail with your feedback. Share with me how you found working with this book; send me examples of writing; tell me what worked and what didn't. Tell me your stories of breathing, stretching, writing.

> *As long as we have stories, we will never be alone.*
> —Sheree Fitch, *There's a Mouse in the House*

Acknowledgments

I am indebted to publisher Mary Macchiusi for her openness to my "first bursts" of creative energy and enthusiasm, for always hearing me out, not to mention her endless patience as I snail along until the work comes to fruition; to Kat Mototsune for her positive vibes, notes, and editing brilliance; to Heather Neilson for hearing me speak it out, typing and fine-tooth–combing.

I owe a thank you to many teachers and students over the years, but most especially to Bernadette Dean and the participants of Somebody's Daughter (2002–2005) in Nunavut, Canada; to Reading for the Love of It (2008, 2009), Toronto, where Mary Wilson said "Yes!" when I first suggested offering a movement/body-based writing workshop; to those first teachers who attended my sessions and so enthusiastically participated and embraced this out-of-the chair approach. To teachers at Shanghai American School; to friend, poet, and writing teacher Amy Young and her students at the Lab School in Washington, DC; to Kristen Moore and class—thank you for allowing me to test-run ideas. To the staff of Great Village Elementary School, Gwen Davies, and all the participants in workshops at the Tatamagouche Centre.

Finally, this book would never have come about without my whole-being eight-year journey into strength, fitness, and wellness in my community at City Fitness, Washington, DC. Lucinda, Dega, Leanne, Rachel, Shawn, Katie, Ellie, Lisa, Tom, Terence, Taj—like all teachers, you ever travel with me. Namaste. Yee-haw!

Suggested Reading

Tania Alexander and Andy Jackson (1995) *The Fitkid Adventure Book: Health-Related Fitness for 5 to 14 Year Olds*

Karen Bellenir (2004) *Fitness Information for Teens: Health Tips about Exercise, Physical Well-Being, and Health Maintenance*

Danielle Bersma (2003) *Yoga Games For Children: Fun And Fitness With Postures, Movements, and Breath*

Dan DeJager (2008) *Adventure Racing Activities for Fun and Fitness*

Ann and Julie Douglas, illustrated by Claudia Davila (2006) *Body Talk: The Straight Facts on Fitness, Nutrition, and Feeling Great About Yourself: A Girl Zone Book*

Katrina Gaede, Alan Lachica, and Doug Werner (2001) *Fitness Training for Girls: A Teen Girl's Guide to Resistance Training, Cardiovascular Conditioning and Nutrition*

Kate Fraser, Judy Tatchell, and Cheryl Evans (1992) *You and Your Fitness and Health*

Harcourt *Health and Fitness Activity Book*, Grades 1–4 (2003)

Thia Luby (2000) *Yoga for Teens: How to Improve Your Fitness, Confidence, Appearance, and Health—And Have Fun Doing It*

Edward Miller (2007) *The Monster Health Book: A Guide to Eating Healthy, Being Active and Feeling Great for Monsters and Kids!*

Michelle H. Nagler (2001) *Get Fit! Eat Right! Be Active!: Girls Guide to Health & Fitness*

Lizzy Rockwell (2004) *The Busy Body Book: A Kid's Guide to Fitness*

Ellen Schwartz, illustrated by Ben Hodson (2003) *I Love Yoga*

Laura Silverstein-Nunn, Alvin Silverstein, and Virginia Silverstein (2002) *My Health: Physical Fitness*

Pat Thomas and Lesley Harker (2004) *My Amazing Body: A First Look at Health and Fitness*

Marlene Wallach, Anna Palma, Grace Norwich, and Monika Roe (2009) *My Life: A Guide to Health & Fitness*

Index